THE LIFE OF MERIASEK

THE LIFE OF MERIASEK
A Medieval Cornish Miracle Play

Newly Translated
by
MARKHAM HARRIS

THE CATHOLIC UNIVERSITY OF AMERICA PRESS
Washington, D. C.

© 1977
The Catholic University of America Press

Library of Congress Cataloging in Publication Data

Beunans Meriasek.   English.
   The life of Meriasek.

    1. Mériasec, Saint, Bp. of Vannes—Drama.
I. Harris, Markham, 1907-   II. Title.
PB2591.B4E5   1977   891.6   77-21760
ISBN 0-8132-0537-9

In Memoriam
Gibson William Harris
1866 - 1941
and
Phyllis Pier Harris
1916 - 1976

PREFACE

As with my translation of the Cornish dramatic trilogy, the *Ordinalia* (1969), the aim of this book is to introduce *Beunans Meriasek* (The Life of Meriasek) to a broader readership than has hitherto had access to what chances to be the only play of its kind (see Introduction) known to have survived the Reformation in Britain. To this end, I have attempted to produce a version of the play which is both responsible and responsive: responsible toward the letter of the Cornish original, responsive to the spirit of the work as a whole.

For all that pertains to the accuracy of the rendering, I am indebted to my colleague, David C. Fowler, and my late wife, Phyllis Pier Harris. Professor Fowler not only supplied the initial impetus for my undertaking a new translation of the *Ordinalia* in the first instance but also devoted the time and attention required for a close reading of the translation of *Beunans Meriasek* in draft. From 1969 onwards, in Washington and in Cornwall, my wife applied her broad knowledge of all that remains to us of medieval Cornish language and literature, and her scholarly exactitude, to a testing and retesting of my results against MS. Peniarth 105 and the transcriptions of it made by Whitley Stokes and R. Morton Nance.

i

Again I am happy to acknowledge a major and continuing debt of gratitude to Mr. H. L. Douch, the curator of the County Museum, Royal Institution of Cornwall, Truro. For what now amounts to a decade, he has astutely and generously put at my disposal the resources of the museum's library, including its invaluable collection of Cornish manuscript materials, to which must be added the benefit of his knowledge of Cornish antiquities and the geography of the county with its bearing upon Cornish place-names, whose presence in *Beunans Meriasek*, as in the *Ordinalia*, constitutes one of the distinctive features of these dramas. I also wish to thank Mr. Roger Penhallurick, the museum's assistant curator, and Miss Angela Broome, its assistant librarian, for their valuable, kind, and long-sustained assistance over, quite literally, the years.

Thanks are likewise due to the Royal Institution of Cornwall for permission to quote from manuscript material in its possession and to Professor Charles Thomas, Camborne, for permission to quote from material on which he holds the copyright.

M. H.

University of Washington
Seattle, Washington

TABLE OF CONTENTS

INTRODUCTION

The play informally known as *Beunans Meriasek,* expanded English translation 'The Life of Saint Meriasek,' survives in a single manuscript discovered in 1862 by W. W. E. Wynne among the Hengwrt MSS at Peniarth, near Towyn, Merionethshire, Wales. Designated MS. Peniarth 105, it is now in the National Library of Wales, Aberystwyth. The manuscript consists of 92 paper leaves measuring *c.* 8½'' x 6''. One leaf is wholly blank, and one is conspicuously short (6¼'' x 6''). Written in a uniform hand, except for the first ten pages of the dialogue and a considerable number of the stage-directions that may have been added later, the work is composed of approximately 4570 lines of stanzaic verse in Middle Cornish. Primary stage-directions and the names of characters are in Latin, while a significant proportion of the secondary stage-directions are in English. Cornish is a Celtic language closely related to Welsh and still more closely to Breton. It was formerly the vernacular of Cornwall, southern Britain's westernmost county.

The discoverer of Peniarth 105 has left to posterity an unaffectedly candid revelation of what, at the outset, he was able to make of his find. His statement, written on a sheet of blue notepaper and

1

pasted to a blank initial page of the MS, reads in part as follows:

I have not an idea what this M.S. is nor in what language it is written. Meriadog & King Conan appear in it. I find in W. Williams' Biographical Dictionary that the former was a chieftain of Derbyshire of the 4th Century who went with an expedition into Brittany...

WWEW.

Dec.
1862

Seven years later the first 36 lines of the Cornish original were printed in *Archaeologia Cambrensis* by the Rev. Robert Williams of Rhydycroesau (Wales). A decade after its discovery, the first and to date the only full edition of the MS was published by Whitley Stokes as *The Life of Saint Meriasek, Bishop and Confessor* (London, 1872). With the appearance of the Stokes edition, featuring his transcription of the MS text set in parallel with a literal English translation, the nature of Wynne's discovery became manifest. He had brought again to light a medieval miracle play, the life of a Breton-Cornish saint in dramatic form, its materials drawn not from the Old and New Testaments as mainly had been those of the Cornish *Ordinalia,* a trilogy of mystery plays, but from ritual, legend, history, and oral tradition. The language of the MS, which Wynne had failed to recognize in the beginning, proved to be a species of Middle Cornish late enough to begin to reflect the eroding pressure of English from England's non-Celtic counties to the east of Cornwall.

As for the two speaking parts singled out by Wynne, Meriasek (his Meriadog) and King Conan, it transpired that the former is the protagonist of the drama, the latter Meriasek's royal kinsman (see no. 7 among the notes assembled at the rear of this volume).

It seems appropriate to introduce an additional consideration at this point. Nothing which has been learned during the century that has passed since the MS was identified, edited, and published has arisen to challenge its singularity, its status as the sole survivor of its kind in Britain. It remains the fact that *Beunans Meriasek* is Britain's only medieval play based on the life of a saint, *i.e.,* miracle play, known to exist. Like the *Ordinalia* in another category, *Meriasek* is unique.

Author and Date of Composition

Without unduly manipulating the available documentary evidence, it might appear to be possible to name an author for *Meriasek* and the year in which he completed his task, the sole requirement being a literal interpretation of the play's colophon. According to this line and a half of Latin positioned below the final line of dialogue in Cornish, the MS was 'finished' (*Finitur*) in the year 1504 by a person styling himself Master (*dominus*), whose surname has come to be read as 'Ton.' There is room for doubt as to the correct rendering of his given name (see n. 112), but the surname and the date were written legibly enough so that only Stokes passes over the second capital letter, a distinct 'T,' in the proper name, his edition rather unaccountably transcribing it as one word printed in all capitals, HADTON, rather than either Had Ton or, as seems more likely, Rad(olphus) Ton. Even so, we still have an individual name of sorts and a date.

Unfortunately, what the colophon seems to assert can only be taken as ambiguous. From the hard evidence it affords, all we can conclude is that, in the year 1504, a cleric whose family name was Ton carried through to completion his copying of most if not all of a codex now known as Peniarth 105. It is not legitimate to interpret the expression *Finitur per* as the equivalent of composed from scratch by the person to whom it refers. A similar limitation applies to the date 1504. The date does establish a limit in time beyond which Peniarth 105 could not have been composed, compiled, or copied, whether in part or as a whole. It fails to determine, however, a limit in time before which no work of any description on what eventually became *Beunans Meriasek* could have been undertaken.

Earlier in the present century, R. Morton Nance, while preparing his bilingual version of the play (typescript, Cornwall County Museum, Truro, n.d.), made a search among the public records of the county for the surname Ton. In a title-deed referring to the first year of Edward VI (1547), he found the name Tonn but was probably right in concluding that it was not necessarily a surname.

Nance also cited one Dominus Ricardus Ton, who was curate of Crowan parish, west Cornwall, in 1537. This citation succeeds in matching both the courtesy title and the last name, howbeit not the disputed first name, furnished by the colophon. Yet even were it possible to disregard the discrepancy between first names and postulate that the two Tons were one and the same, we would be nearer to confirming the identity of the manuscript's chief copyist but no nearer to discovering its author or authors. One also remembers how inconsequential the matter of exclusive proprietorship in a literary work would have been likely to seem during the Middle Ages, when responsibility for original composition was so often lost in anonymity or blurred by silent appropriation, much as the worked stone of a derelict church was wont to find its eventual place in the wall of a private garden, sometimes nearby, sometimes at a far remove.

In his book, *Christian Antiquities of Camborne* (St. Austell, 1967), Professor Charles Thomas adopts a broader and more flexible approach to the question of author and date. He writes as follows (Ch. II, p. 23):

> If BM was written or (more accurately) compiled in the late 15th century, its author is likely to have had some connection with the great collegiate church of Glasney at Penryn, the main intellectual centre of west Cornwall and a known focus for the production of such miracle plays. [In other than British usage, the other plays assumed to be ascribable to Glasney would be termed mystery plays.] Now a connection about this time between Camborne and Glasney *is* known. Dr. John Nans, who had been collated as Provost of Glasney in 1497, went to Camborne as Rector in 1501, exchanging positions with Master Alexander Penhylle or Penhale, who left Camborne to go to Glasney. Penhylle had been Rector of the next door parish of Illogan from 1493 to 1500, had only been at Camborne for a year, and had been a Prebend of Glasney since 1495.

Professor Thomas' views are of value for several reasons. As the title of his book-length study indicates, west Cornwall's well-known settlement of Camborne and its environs are at the focus of his inquiry; they are likewise the predominant setting for those episodes in the play which deal with Meriasek's visit to Cornwall from his native Brittany. Furthermore, it can readily be deduced from internal evidence that the playwright, whoever he may have been, was familiar with Cornwall's geography, particularly with that of west Cornwall and the Camborne area, while his sense of

4

Breton geography seems dependent on reading only. Professor Thomas is far from claiming that Dr. Nans or Master Penhylle compiled *Beunans Meriasek,* much less composed it. But he does suggest, and rightly, that either of these two men was in all probability qualified to have had a hand in it, say as editor or adapter, between 1495 and 1501, by virtue of capabilities that must have included an acquaintance not merely with medieval Latin and liturgy but also with sacred legend, the environment, traditions, and history of the church and parish of Camborne, to which should be added those of Glasney Collegiate Church at Penryn (see n. 106). They presumably possessed these qualifications; they may have had the ability to read, write, and speak Cornish, together with some feel for the history of the very early medieval church and the late Roman empire in the West which the play reveals. For a further consideration of Glasney as the presumptive alma mater of Cornwall's medieval dramatists, the reader is referred to Thurstan C. Peter, *The History of Glasney Collegiate Church* (Camborne, 1903) and Markham Harris, *The Cornish Ordinalia* (Washington, D. C., 1969).

Aside from the witness of the colophon and what little may be inferred from scattered bits of internal evidence that allude, for instance, to firearms and minted coins (see the Notes, *passim*), even an approximate dating of the play must await the kind of study already afforded the *Ordinalia* (David C. Fowler, "The Date of the Cornish *Ordinalia*," *Mediaeval Studies,* XXIII (Toronto, 1961), pp. 91-125). Meanwhile, the informed consensus places the extant version of *Meriasek* toward the close of the 15th century, about three generations later than the *Ordinalia,* one generation earlier than the date of the colophon. As to whether one or another episode of the MS might have existed in dramatic form before 1475, for instance, there is no present basis for either flat affirmation or denial.

Sources

The documentary sources of the play are to be found for the most part in the divine service manuals of medieval Brittany. Although the precise dating of these liturgical books is out of the question and their origin a matter of conjecture, thanks to the persevering labors of Canon Gilbert H. Doble (*The Saints of Cornwall,* Part I, The Dean and Chapter of Truro, 1960) it is possible to specify with reasonable confidence where the author could have found a fairly detailed basis for the Breton episodes of his play.

It is convenient to begin with a 17th century work by the Breton Dominican, Albert Le Grand, whose *Vies des saints de la Bretagne armorique* (1636) provides a Life of St. Meriasek. While Le Grand's book itself of course was of too late date to have been used in the composition of *Beunans Meriasek,* it is otherwise with the sources of Meriasek's biography which Le Grand acknowledges at the close of his account of the saint. He gives as his major sources the Proper of Saints of Vennes (Vannes) and "an old manuscript Legendary kept in the Church of Saint John Traoun-Meriadec, called 'of the Finger' in the parish of Plou'gaznou, diocese of Treguer (Treguier)." *Traoun-Meriadec* means 'Valley of Meriasek'; the Church of Saint Jean Traoun-Meriadec is now known as the Chapel of Saint-Jean-du-Doigt (of the Finger) situated near the coast of north central Brittany, one of the regions that still retain evidences of St. Meriasek's cult, including what Canon Doble describes as "a seventeenth century statue...representing the saint in cope and mitre, with crozier, in the act of blessing, and a silver reliquary in the form of a bust within which is a portion of the saint's skull."

We need go no further into Albert Le Grand's sources than the Proper of Saints of Vannes in order to find a broad foundation for the Breton episodes of the play. The three lessons of the second nocturn at Matins on the feast of Meriadocus closely anticipate the dramatic action. Lesson I specifies that the saint was a descendant of Conan, 'King' of Brittany; that his was a pious childhood; that once come to man's estate, he renounced the world and withdrew to a place near the castle of Pontivy. Lessons II and III summarize the remainder of Meriasek's life with its miracles, its special concern for the sick and the poor, and the saint's traditional reluctance to exchange (*c.* the year 659, according to Lesson III) the role of hermit for that of bishop. Le Grand does not follow the Proper of Saints of Vannes in supplying a date for Meriasek's consecration as bishop. He does, however, supply another of what have been termed *précisions pseudo-historiques,* placing the saint's birth at about "the year of grace 758," a figure which the Bollandist Fathers were to regard as intended to read either 578 or 587.

The fact that Albert Le Grand's other principal authority for his Life of Meriasek, namely, the old manuscript Legendary kept in the Church of Saint John Traoun-Meriadec, has disappeared makes the history of its literary genealogy as traced by Canon Doble (*op. cit.,* pp. 122-23) too intricate for full exposition here. But in brief, Doble's search moves from the vanished legendary of St. John Traoun-Meriadec to that of the diocese of Treguier to which St. John's church belonged. From that legendary he was led to the discovery in the Bibliothèque Nationale at Paris of a long-unknown manuscript (MSS Lat., fonds franc., No. 22321). Doble identifies his discovery as a 17th century copy of a 15th century Latin Life of Meriasek once a part of the diocesan legendary of Treguier which is presumed to have been destroyed during the French Revolution. He reproduces the entire Latin text of his find as an appendix to his biographical study of the saint and in a systematic comparison of the recovered *Vita* with the play demonstrates their close, sustained similarity and at more than a few points their identity. When, in addition, Doble concludes his source-analysis with the opinion that the Paris *Vita* "is a copy of that in the old manuscript legendary of Vannes, now lost," he may be pushing inference a little too hard although he is not without the support of textual evidence for his view (*op. cit.,* p. 123). What sustains his general position, however moot certain of its details may be, is the undoubted community of liturgical texts, whether on the Continent or in medieval Britain, united by the Roman Church and the Latin language.

There was a time earlier in the present century when at least two students of the play were convinced that its Cornish episodes, as well as those set in Brittany, once had a written source or sources. Canon Doble accepted the evidence of a stage-direction which should have read *Hic filius Mulieris cuiusdam ut invenitur in miraculis de beate marie pompabit* 'Here the son of a certain woman, as found in the miracles of Blessed Mary, shall parade' as reading according to Stokes in his edition:...*ut invenitur in miraculis de beato mereadoco* 'as found in the miracles of the

Blessed *Meriasek'* (italics added). The style in which Stokes clothes his translation of the Latin *miraculis de beato mereadoco, viz.,* 'the Miracles of Blessed Meriasek,' makes obvious his assumption that the title of a book was involved. Reasoning more circumspectly toward the same end, Cornwall's former scholar and ethnic enthusiast, Henry Jenner, argued that the Cornish strand of the play's action was derived by analogy with the manuscript life of one or another patron saint of parishes in the vicinity of Camborne, such as St. Illogan (see Master Penhylle above) or St. Uny (Henry Jenner, "King Teudar," in *Tre, Pol and Pen,* Cornish Association, London, 1928).

But as Professor Thomas has pointed out (*op. cit.,* pp. 24-5), even the oral traditions concerning this pair of holy men are scant at best, whereas a written Life of another neighboring and, like Meriasek, both a Breton and a Cornish saint, *i.e.,* St. Fingar or Gwinear, has not only survived the destructive hostility of the Reformation, but it also bears an author's name and has a provenance. The authorship is credited to a man in holy orders named Anselm (not to be confused with St. Anselm, Archbishop of Canterbury from 1093 to 1109). He is thought to have composed his Life of St. Gwinear, of which a version is to be found in the monumental *Acta sanctorum* of the Bollandists, about 1300. Canon Doble refers to what he terms the original MS as having been in the library of the Abbey of Saint-Victor, Paris. In his biographical study of Meriasek (*op. cit.,* p. 130) he remarks: "It must surely be more than a coincidence that in Cornwall the parish of Gwinear adjoins that of Camborne, while in Brittany S. Gwinear and S. Meriadoc are honored in the same parish."

Whatever else it may imply, the geographical pairing of these saints in Cornwall and in Brittany does prompt a comparison of their Lives. Certain similarities become evident, yet it is doubtful whether they are not outweighed by differences. Common attributes or incidents include a royal lineage and persecution by a tyrant, which, together with faith healing, are part of the conventional furniture of medieval hagiography. On the other hand, Anselm has brought to his *Vita Guigneri* such an exuberance of pious fancy (a leaf-boat that transits the Irish Sea, a cow which achieves resurrection from a mere heap of bones and hide and whose descendants give three times as much milk as other, less charismatic cows) and such sacred, arithmetic exactitude (the 770 men and 7 bishops, no more, no less, who accompany St. Gwinear on one of his more mundane voyages to Cornwall) as to underline contrast rather than comparison.

On balance, it seems most probable that the Cornish episodes of the play have their origin in oral tradition, a conclusion to which the utter silence concerning Cornwall of the Breton documentary sources lends mute support. If written sources ever existed, no trace of them has been found.

For its non-Celtic episodes, located in or near Rome and centered upon interactions between Pope Silvester I and Constantine the Great, Peniarth 105 is extensively indebted to some compilation of tradition, very likely the *Legenda Aurea*, the 13th c. anthology compiled by Jacobus de Voragine, archbishop of Genoa. Very popular and hence influential in its own day, its claim that so pivotal an event as the conversion to Christianity of the Roman emperor Constantine I was accomplished by St. Silvester came to have wide acceptance during the Middle Ages. The play adopts the Jacobus account of the Conversion of Constantine and dramatizes it quite faithfully as to what happens, the order in which it happens, where it happens, and, in certain instances, closely paraphrases the language through which the action is conveyed by Jacobus. A few examples will serve to illustrate this.

Like the Emperor Tiberius in the *Ordinalia,* Constantine is stricken with leprosy for his sins, witting and unwitting, against the Christian faith. Once he has canceled, however, the horrific plan to cure his disease by immersion in the warm blood of 3000 slaughtered children and resigns himself to die of leprosy, he is visited in a dream by Saints Peter and Paul. When, earlier in the action, Constantine is represented as authorizing a general massacre of Christians, Pope Silvester and his clergy go into hiding on Mt. Soracte north of Rome (see n. 37). Just after the leper's mask is removed from his face as Constantine emerges from the water of baptism, Peniarth 105 supplies a non-dramatic passage in Latin which echoes *Legenda Aurea* at the same point (see n. 49).

In a later episode, the play again levies upon *The Golden Legend* for its dramatization of another Silvester incident, his taming of a

9

dragon, although on this occasion the playwright's borrowings from source are less literal and more selective. He retains the general drift, but where, for instance, Jacobus specifies the use of a pair of lanterns to light the way into the monster's lair, the drama calls for a cross and a lantern. On stage, the dragon's symbolic meaning is left to implication; in the *Legenda,* the fearsome creature embodies Satan himself: "and thou, Satan, await His coming in this place!"

By contrast, Peniarth 105 greatly expands its dramatization of Mary and the Woman's Son as found in *The Golden Legend.* Where Jacobus supplies a compact, unembellished narrative, employing a minimum of characters (three) and incident, the playwright develops around the legendary core an interlude which totals 646 lines. It adds upwards of a dozen speaking parts, among them King Massen (see below) and a number of auxiliary incidents such as hunting scenes, a battle between King Massen and a local tyrant reminiscent of Teudar (see above), a pagan votive scene, and passages of low comedy among the tyrant and his discontented underlings.

Beunans Meriasek as Drama

Among those who have not only studied this unique medieval work but have also left a record of their reactions to it, there has been little or no disposition to deny it a measure of such literary virtues as vitality, charm, humor, quickness, and beyond all else, variety. At the same time, no one has yet been found to claim that Peniarth 105 possesses dramatic unity or even epic unity, the unity of the hero. Whitley Stokes, the original editor, offers no purely literary opinions whatever. Henry Jenner observes with bluff literalness that the only pin which keeps its principal strands of plot together is the feckless anachronism by which Pope Silvester, an historical figure who died in 335, is made to issue bulls for the consecration as bishop of the legendary Meriasek, whose birth is not presumed to have occurred before 578 at the earliest. Morton Nance, whatever were his views on the subject, may be said to have voted with his pen, inasmuch as his transcription and translation abandon the sequence of the MS, dividing it into three semi-

10

independent units: Life of St. Meriasek, Life of St. Silvester, and the playlet or interlude of Mary and the Woman's Son. Writing as recently as 1967, Professor Thomas observes (*op. cit.*, p. 23): "Most medieval mystery or miracle plays disregard the classic unities of the theatre, but the structure of BM is not just a simple sandwich; on this analogy, it would be a ten-tiered layer cake."

The solidarity of this consensus, whether rendered by silence, gesture, or word, can hardly be questioned. What can be questioned, perhaps, is the soundness of the verdict in light of the full evidence which the play provides.

Under unhurried examination, the action of *Beunans Meriasek* as a whole, seemingly so naive, restless, jerky, kaleidoscopic, gradually resolves into something decidedly more appropriate to its nature and purpose. It becomes antiphonal. The plot structure is three-fold, the two major strands being those of Meriasek and of Silvester. The third and lesser strand is a play within a play, the interlude of Mary and the Woman's Son, traditionally regarded either as a means of lengthening Day II of the performance, which would otherwise be out of balance with Day I, or of puffing the local cult of Mary of Camborne. Either or both of these motives may have influenced the final result, yet neither of them should be allowed to obscure the presence in the over-all action of patent correspondences, parallels, homologous parts which promote unity and symmetry despite interruptions of sequence, changes of place, and gaps in time.

In the Meriasek strand, the saint tames a fearsome wolf; in the Silvester strand, that saint subdues a horrendous dragon. In the Meriasek plot, the saint takes refuge under a massive granite outcropping from the pursuit of Teudar, a pagan tyrant; in the Silvester plot, the saintly pope takes refuge on Mt. Soracte from the murderous soldiers of the pagan emperor, Constantine. As Bishop of Vannes, Meriasek heals two lepers; as Bishop of Rome, Silvester heals only the one leper, but that one is Constantine the Great.

These and other correspondences of event are reinforced by counterparts of attainment and identity. As the action unfolds, Meriasek's career is seen to parallel that of Silvester, except for the latter's accession to the papal throne. In order come the religious vocation, the education, the priesthood, the traditional reluctance to assume the episcopal mitre, the miracles of healing, the ultimate sainthood. Further, the interlude of Mary and the Woman's Son not only returns to the cult of the Virgin stressed in the Meriasek plot but also introduces a king named Massen, at first glance appearing to identify no more than the petty ruler of an unspecified domain. Such an identification, however, takes no account of the linguistic, legendary, and historical dimensions of the name. King Massen appears as Macsen Wledig in a Welsh tale of the 13th c., *The Dream of King Macsen*, wherein, as the Roman emperor Maximus, he comes to Britain and marries Helen of the Hosts. Through popular confusion of Helen of the Hosts with Helen or Helena, the mother of Constantine the Great, Macsen (Maximus) becomes the father of Constantine. When there is added to this skein of once-credited interrelationships the name of Conan Meriadec as a principal associate of Maximus during that emperor's invasion of Brittany (see n. 7), the integration of the drama's sub-plot, Mary and the Woman's Son, with both of its main plots becomes manifest to a modern eye, whether or not its medieval author was aware of the connective tissue that lies below the surface of his composition.

For those whose literary taste inclines toward the classical, the play's double deployment of time, the one dramatic, the other quasi-historical, is likely to prove disconcerting on both counts. As theatre, it reads as if Aristotle had never observed that tragedy "endeavors, as far as possible, to confine its action within the limits of a single revolution of the sun" (Twining's translation). By this standard, *Meriasek*, which manages to confine its action within the vague span of the saint's lifetime, fails dismally. But Peniarth 105 is not a tragedy in either the classical or medieval sense of the term. It is a miracle play, the enacted life-history of a saint, for which an Aristotelian compression of dramatic time would be inappropriate if not crippling.

The play's use of historical time must seem utterly indefensible, unless on the assumption that Meriasek rivals the Biblical patriarchs by living for centuries: at a minimum from several decades before 335 (death of Pope Silvester I) to several decades after 578, the earliest date of his birth offered by Breton hagiography; at a maximum, from the era of Constantine the Great (4th c.) to the first minting of the silver groat (see n. 84), in the 14th c. By the latter computation, Meriasek succeeded in living longer than Methuselah's 969 years (*Gen.* 5:27).

But this is to reason on several not necessarily congruent levels. One of these is the secular, viewing history as a study of verifiable and finite time process; another the legendary, as unverifiable, if finite, time process; a third, the sacerdotal, involving matters of belief, absolute and unverifiable as the term is being employed in the present context. For the greater part, *Beunans Meriasek* moves on the sacerdotal level, its progress steeped in the wonders of divine revelation and intervention. Within the span of its priestly episodes, the timelessness of a medieval heaven looks down upon the doings of mankind on earth. The Logos of *John* 1: 1-5 is numbered among the drama's speaking parts, his celestial home assigned a station, as is that of Hell, on the perimeter of the Cornish theatre-in-the-round (see below, Staging). Under the action of so powerful a solvent, temporal limits and distinctions tend to dissolve, hushing all protest against anachronism: "Then said the Jews unto him, Thou art not yet fifty years old, and hast thou seen Abraham? Jesus said unto them, Verily, verily, I say unto you, Before Abraham was, I am." (*John* 8: 56-58)

The play may appear to make as free with place as it does with time, moving at will between Brittany, Cornwall, and Italy, yet the unifying ties, correspondences, interconnections among physically separated territories are so abundant that no more than a sampling of the evidence can be included here. To begin with, there is the name, Brittany, *i.e.*, Little Britain or Lesser Britain. It witnesses the early medieval migrations of the Celtic inhabitants of Cornwall and Wales across the narrow seas between what are now England and France. Former regional designations, such as Dumnonia in northern Brittany and Cornouailles in the south of the peninsula, attest where the island *émigrés* settled in significant numbers. Dumnonia was the Roman name for Cornwall and Devon, present-day England's contiguous southwestern counties. Linguistic ties are no less abundant. Not only was Latin the learned tongue common to all three countries, but also what are termed the Brythonic group of Celtic languages — Welsh, Breton,

13

and Cornish — were cognate, the affinity between Breton and Cornish particularly having been close enough to provide a measure of mutual intelligibility for both speakers and writers of these dialects. Underpinning the whole was a common religion, dominantly homogeneous throughout the geographical setting of *Meriasek*. It is true that the saint himself displays an enthusiasm for hermitic extremes of asceticism and isolation from human society that suggest certain practices of Celtic Christianity, but neither in over-all substance nor atmosphere does the play reflect a faith other than that of medieval Roman Catholicism.

To turn from the concerns of action and setting to those of characterization is to move toward the relatively simple and straightforward. As has been seen, the question of who figures like King Conan, Teudar, and King Massen are, what the full range of their respective identities may encompass, has not proved easy. What they are, as apprehended through their voiced thoughts, words, and deeds, gives less pause. This is so because the playwright shows comparatively little disposition to depart from his known sources of either plot or portraiture and because his dialogue, for which he alone seems to have been responsible with only trifling exceptions (see, for example, n. 47) is consistently economical and unambiguous, even when it waxes contentious, abusive, or merely playful. Repetitive it can be, upon occasion, and at times rather pedestrian, but rarely, if ever, complicated or long-winded.

The principal among principals, Meriasek, has the clarity, uniformity, and, in consequence, the predictability of a crystal, appearing to change only as the angle of the light upon him changes. He is inescapably a Christ-figure, as much by virtue of his steady brightness as by his miracles of healing or his devotion to the Father's business from childhood or his stilling of the waters of the English Channel. While on stage, he lives in the noonday sun, registering shadowless innocence. Not until after his holy dying, as posthumously recounted by the dean of Vannes cathedral in a messenger speech to an assemblage of Breton lords, does his image assume a slightly darker, elegiac hue.

Such other principals as Silvester and Constantine are similarly monolithic and, like Meriasek, humorless. They also lack his length of exposure on stage and his luminosity. Much the same thing applies to Teudar, save that he is endowed with a broader range of capacities and has humor, howbeit at his own expense. In the matter of range, there is the Teudar who rages, who out-Herods Herod; there is also the Teudar who debates with Meriasek on the basic dogmas of the Faith, upholding his side with point as well as vigor. At times the self-assured chieftain, the imperator, Teudar sinks at other times into buffoonery and slap-stick, during which he retains his vigor if not his dignity.

Those familiar with the hazards of imaginative composition in general will scarcely find it surprising that the author(s) of what became Peniarth 105 may well have succeeded in giving to one or another of the minor characters an illusion of reality, an unlabored authority of fictional presence, not to be found among the more major characters. Something of this kind seems as true of *Meriasek* as of the *Ordinalia* (*cf.* Harris, *op. cit.*, pp. xiv-xvi). The latter work has its venal crozier-bearer, its adolescent jailor's boy; the former, such minor yet free-hand creations as Meriasek's grammar master, the doctor's apprentice Jenkin, and a series of brief yet telling roles which the MS labels simply *Domesticus* or, more often, *Calo*, with meanings that include, depending upon context, 'native,' 'household servant,' 'drudge,' 'menial.' In only one instance (see n. 83) is a menial given a proper name and then only in the mouth of another character.

Unencumbered by responsibility toward his sources, the dramatist gives evidence of having sketched these lesser people from life, from personal observation, not excluding, perhaps, observation of himself. He envisions the Grammar Master as a man who dismisses his alma mater (see n. 4) with a pun, who limbers his Latinist's tongue with wine, whose livelihood depends more on keeping a boarding house than a school. Nevertheless, this man is quick to recognize the special quality of the new boy, Meriasek, and is less impressed by the newcomer's high lineage than by his lofty spiritual vocation before which all but the most essential house rules shall and should bend. It has required fewer than thirty lines to draw this miniature in mixed black and white which yields the gray of humankind.

Apprentice Jenkin, although a cruder, less appealing figure

than the Grammar Master, is presented with like economy. From first to last, he conceives of his physician master as part quack, part lecher, part confidence man, saying nothing to soften the implication that all medical men of the day were of the same stripe superimposed upon a background of pretense, greed, and ignorance. The further implication is, of course, that Jenkin regards himself as a person of opposite stripe. Final judgment is left to an audience for whom doctor and apprentice, whatever their respective merits or demerits, are pagans, lost to the great truth that all genuine healing is from God alone.

If the Grammar Master and the 'Sorcerer's' Apprentice may rightly be viewed as in some sort vehicles of author opinion as well as examples of efficient character-drawing on a small scale, the same can be said of those yet more miniaturized working parts, the Native and the Menial. Through their brief, occasional presences and voices, the play projects a number of themes colored by humor at one time sly, at another, bawdy, at a third, grim. The native of Camborne who gives Meriasek his first bit of local orientation soon amiably discloses his built-in preference for ale or wine, when he can get it, over the saint's ascetic and exclusive allegiance to water. One of the menials of the Silvester plot not only brags about his zeal in rounding up young children for Constantine's prospective immersion in their cleansing blood, he also boasts that he has partially equalized his tally of doomed captives by casual begettings in the course of his mission. It is, moreover, the same character who says to a self-confessed Christian about to be martyred for his faith: "Hold your tongue! Leave it to me to save myself. When have you seen an unclaimed soul in this world? Though heaven's gates are shut, hell still gapes wide. Which way I go is all one to me." In its medieval setting, this has to be one of the play's most terse and chilling speeches (ll. 1252-57).

Staging

The key to a general understanding of how medieval Cornwall's drama was staged on its native ground lies in the configuration of the Cornish open-air theatre in the round. Since the rounds are essentially circular earthworks once surrounded by a ditch, the contention that a number of them began as strongholds, defenses against enemy incursions by land and more particularly by sea, has merit. But with time, even these were converted to such comparatively bloodless activities as wrestling and play production.

Today Cornwall possesses, among others, a prime surviving example of a medieval playing place (Cor. *plen-an-guary*) located on high ground inland from the sea and from Perranporth, a popular summer resort on the county's north coast. However much it may have been altered by gravitation, weather, and man through the centuries, Perran (Piran) Round, which was refurbished as recently as 1969, forms a large, shallow, grass-carpeted bowl situated on a level site and still encircled by the remains of a dry moat or ditch. The record testifies that on the outside the bowl formerly rose an average of 12 ft. from the bottom of the ditch, the rim forming a rampart several feet wide. From this rampart, an inner bank at present affording a rough-and-ready accommodation for spectators slopes down on all sides to the circular stage, whose diameter averages approximately 130 feet. The result is an unobstructed playing area (Lat. *platea* or *placea*, Cor. *plen*, Engl. 'plain') in excess of 13,000 sq. ft. The bank is cut through on the north and south, the latter cut now serving as the main entrance to the theatre. The stage is more or less level except for a spoon-shaped depression lying in the eastern quadrant of the circle. The original purpose of the depression, which has come to be known as the Devil's Spoon, has long been a matter of conjecture.

A specific link between the basic design of an amphitheatre like Perran Round and an envisioned performance of *Beunans Meriasek* before a medieval audience is provided by a pair of schematic drawings appended to the text of Days I and II in Peniarth 105. The drawings position on a circle the stations or platforms assigned to the regions of Heaven to the east and Hell to the north, which figure in both Days of the play, and a few leading or else ubiquitous characters. The diagrams also specify that the representation of a chapel shall occupy centre stage throughout Day I, St. Samson's church at Dol (Brittany) taking its place during Day II (but see n. 78).

A second link between theatre and play is created by those stage-directions that call upon a character to make his entrance by 'going down' to the stage, his exit by 'going up' from it. The initial instance of a descent in *Meriasek* (occurring between ll. 141 and 142) reads: *Descendat solus ad capellam* 'Let him (Meriasek) go down alone to the chapel.' That this language is functionally precise can be demonstrated by its conformity to the general plan of a round and to the schematic drawing for Day I of the play. The schoolboy Meriasek is directed to leave the Grammar Master's station, as shown in the diagram to be either on the inner slope or, more likely, the rampart of the round's southeasterly sector, and descend to the chapel in the middle of the *platea*. In a round the size of Perran, the sight of a small boy executing his solitary, self-directed errand of piety could hardly fail as spectacle, and how much does it matter as either image or concept that the chapel toward which he proceeds cannot literally be that of Mary of Camborne in Cornwall? The time is not ripe, since the future bishop, confessor (champion of the Faith), and saint is still a child at school in Brittany. An early illustration of stage movement both down and up, within the compass of a single speech by Teudar, comes just after his first encounter with the mature Meriasek in Cornwall (ll. 942-55). The tyrant's rapid shuttle between the plain and his station seems calculated to produce a comic effect on this occasion. (Readers who are interested in a more extended discussion of Cornish theatres-in-the-round and in matters of medieval staging, including the relation between stage levels and the parish church as a setting for religious drama, are invited to consult Richard Southern, *The Medieval Theatre in the Round* (1957), particularly Ch. 11, and Harris, *op. cit.*, pp. xvii-xxiii.)

It remains to be mentioned that in a single, unique instance a combined stage-direction and production note surviving in Peniarth 105 simultaneously refers to an individual member of the cast by name and furnishes a clue as to the minimum physical dimensions of the stage required to implement the action it anticipates. The rubric, which marks a change of scene just after l. 1865 (see nn. 50, 51) reads in the original English of the MS as follows: *And John ergudyn aredy a horse bakke yᵗ was yᵉ Justis wᵗ constantine ffor to play yᵉ marchant.* 'And John Ergudyn, who was the Justice with Constantine, on horseback ready to play the merchant.'

18

Editors and Translators

To date, the only edition of *Beunans Meriasek* to reach publication is that of Whitley Stokes in 1872 (see above). Stokes produced an invaluable pioneer work, consisting of a conscientious transcription of the Cornish original and a literal English translation of it, plus an introduction, notes, and list of corrections, all emphasizing the linguistic aspect of Peniarth 105. Like Edwin Norris, who produced the first and thus far the only thorough-going edition of the *Ordinalia* (*The Ancient Cornish Drama*, Oxford, 1859), Stokes was primarily concerned with preserving a major addition to the surviving body of written Cornish, a language whose spontaneous life had died away into silence toward the close of the 18th c.

It was with the idea of reversing this trend toward permanent extinction of Cornish as a living language that R. Morton Nance, at work in Cornwall during the first half of the present century, set himself to renovate what had been preserved of Middle Cornish by a process of regularization, particularly of spelling and word division, which came to be known as Unified Cornish. In the course of his labors, Nance systematically converted known Middle Cornish texts, including Peniarth 105, into Unified Cornish, partly in order to resolve cruxes and furnish emendations. Whatever differences of opinion there may be concerning the net value of Nance's reform of the language, there can be no question about the contributions he made to resolving enigmas of meaning in *Meriasek*. Before his death in 1959, Nance and his collaborator, A. S. D. Smith, had issued extracts in Unified Cornish and English from the extant literature, among them being the episode of Adam and Seth (*Ordinalia*, Day I) and Silvester and the Dragon (*Beunans Meriasek*, Day II).

The translation which follows makes no attempt to duplicate, much less rival, the essentially linguistic accomplishments of Stokes or Nance and Smith. Without the work of these able precursors, it would have been far more difficult to undertake a new rendering, the first in prose, which seeks to give the play a more vivid profile, to afford its architectural and verbal features greater clarity and accessibility, and, within responsible limits, to find for the native range and variety of the Cornish a correlative in English insofar as such a thing is ever possible.

19

Here Begins the Play
of
THE LIFE OF SAINT MERIASEK, BISHOP AND CONFESSOR (Part I)[1]

(Here Meriasek's father shall parade.)

MERIASEK'S FATHER

I am the Duke of Brittany,[2] scion of the blood royal, my authority
in this kingdom second only to that of his sovereign majesty, King
Conan himself.[3] As his kinsman, I hold place above the gentle and
the rude alike, my name respected among the nobility.

We have an only son named Meriasek. At this time I desire to
send him to school that he may learn those things that are good for
a man to know. If it please God, it is my heartfelt wish to elevate
him to a position from which he will hold sway over wide dominions.

MOTHER

Your plan to advance the boy, my lord, is well conceived. Already
letter-perfect in his reading, if now he could acquire learning, it
would be splendid and a future source of honor. Do you want to go
away to school, dear son? Tell us.

MERIASEK

Ah, Father, Mother, study and learning are like food and drink to me. To understand the Scriptures, to be able, as well, to distinguish between good and evil is ever my wish.

FATHER

God bless you, Meriasek, always fervent-minded, keen to learn what's best!

Messenger, go at once with my beloved son to the master of the grammar school.

FIRST MESSENGER

Your command shall be obeyed, my lord. I know where the master lives, and I also know that he is wonderfully good with children. Whenever you are ready, Meriasek, we will set out.

MERIASEK

Father, I ask your blessing and yours too, Mother, that I may have grace the better to learn profitable things as long as I live. Your blessings mean more to me than the wealth of all the world.

FATHER

God's blessing and mine be upon you, precious son, from this day forward. As long as you live you shall never come short of your purpose because of me.

And now, squire, accompany my son to school and watch over him faithfully there, a place where you also, perhaps, can learn much that is worthwhile.

MOTHER

May the blessing of Mary be yours, my son, and my own blessing always. I will kiss you on the lips, for it is right that we should love you thus dearly. I trust in God above that when we, your parents, are old and feeble, you will carry on by the light of our precepts.

DUKE'S SQUIRE

Let's be on our way to school, Meriasek. I'm one who still can't read, not a word and don't even know my letters. May the good God watch over us.

(Here the schoolmaster shall parade.)

MASTER

I am a master of grammar, having taken my degree at Bonilapper,[4] a university of modest size. I have a solid background in sacred texts, and when my skin is full of wine, I'm minded to speak Latin, Latin exclusively.[5]

FIRST MESSENGER

Honor to you, worthy master, and always deep respect. None other than Duke Conan has sent his son to you, my dear doctor, to study under you. Teach him well, and you will be rewarded.

MASTER

You need harbor no doubts on that head, messenger. I shall so teach him that this land will not contain his equal as a grammarian.

Come, sit down nicely among the children, Meriasek, and look at your books or else recite some little thing. Learning won't ever come easy nor my fees either.

FIRST SCHOLAR

God help me, A, B, C. That one at the end of the line is D. I don't know any more in the book.[6] Faith, I've only been in the school since late last night. After I eat, Master, I'll do the best I can to learn more.

SECOND SCHOLAR

E, S, T, that's *est*. What comes next, I'm not quite sure. Master, don't beat me! it won't improve me. But if I could have a bite of something, I'd do better.

MASTER

You must learn more with your companions, and when you've a mind to, go and eat. Go with the others, Meriasek, my dear, for you're still tender in years. The young love food, and on that love my livelihood depends.

MERIASEK

While not meaning to displease you, Master, I would point out that today is surely Friday, a day on which it is good to forgo a meal and think of the soul. For the sake of the Passion which Jesus underwent for us, I wish to fast today. And on every Friday in the year, I'd much rather pray than eat.

I will go to the chapel, to Christ who shed his blood, to make my prayer, and to Mary his mother, before I eat or drink anything. That is my way.

MASTER

Follow the path your heart has chosen, my boy. I now see plainly that you are destined for saintliness. Go and come, Meriasek, as seems best to you. As far as possible you shall be free from restrictions at all times.

(Let Meriasek go down alone to the chapel.)

MERIASEK

(In the chapel)

Jesus, lord of heaven and earth, to you I make my prayer. Jesus, Lord, guard me from the tempting of devils and enable me to serve you faithfully all the days of my life. To your worship, Jesus, I give body and spirit, mind and strength, humbly praying that I may never be turned toward the pleasures of this world.

Mary, Queen of Heaven, whose milk did nourish the Christ, intercede for me, a learner. Sweet Mary, pray for me that the wicked devil may never have power over me, nor the world, my other enemy. The evils of the flesh I shall subdue by vigil and by penance. In youth and age, ever to please Christ is my hope and my desire.

(And then he returns to the master.)

(Here King Conan shall parade.)

23

KING CONAN

I am Conan, King of Brittany,[7] sole monarch of this domain. On the advice of my nobles, I go forthwith to the duke of the realm, head of our knightly order and my closest blood relation. There has been proposed to us a grand alliance through the marriage of the duke's son, Meriasek, to the daughter of a great sovereign,[8] none greater under heaven.

FIRST LORD

Meriasek is a prudent young man, likewise polite, and modest beyond any youth in the kingdom. I venture to say, peerless lord, that if she were to be found, he would deserve an emperor's daughter for his consort.

SECOND LORD

Meriasek is beloved. Much good is reported of him in this country. I advise you in all seriousness that I have not heard tell of his like nor of his superior in virtue anywhere.

MERIASEK

If it meets with your approval, Master, I ask permission to return home that I may again see my father and mother. You have taught me excellently well; it is right that I bless you for it.

MASTER

May Christ bless you, Meriasek, as do I and that most heartily! You are full of blessedness. Indeed, my school has never had your equal in learning or in virtue.
(*Meriasek goes down with the squire and returns to his father.*)

MERIASEK

Joyful greetings and my respects to you, revered father, and to you, honored mother, now and ever! I ask your unreserved blessing. Now that the Holy Spirit has enlightened my understanding, I have been able to perfect my studies, thanks be to Christ, king of the angels.

FATHER

Welcome home, Meriasek, my unstinted blessing is yours! If through leaving us you have been allowed to make such fine progress in your studies, I am only the better pleased.

Knights, prepare yourselves for the arrival of his majesty, King Conan, this very evening.

MOTHER

Christ's blessing be upon you, Meriasek, and your mother's blessing always! From what we have heard about you, you deserve both welcome and honor for your excellence. Lord, how you are praised — and how freely — all over Brittany!

KING CONAN

(To the duke)

Our respectful salutations to you, highly esteemed sir. Inasmuch as you are, worthy duke, a person of consequence and, moreover, a kinsman, I have come here to confer with you. Greetings also to you, Lady, and to that cherished son who is by your side, my close relation, Meriasek.

MERIASEK'S FATHER

Welcome, my worshipful liege, welcome here, truly welcome, you and your entire retinue! This sight of you in my castle will gladden me throughout the coming year.

MERIASEK'S MOTHER

You are welcome here, our sovereign. We are deeply gratified by your presence. Though the father who reared me were now to enter my house, he could never be more welcome than are you.

MERIASEK

Welcome, royal sire, our leader and our chief, meriting our respect since it is by your guidance we are ruled, high and low alike.

KING CONAN

Much thanks to you all! Before we part, I wish to broach a certain matter that is to the benefit and advantage of Meriasek, my next of kin.

MERIASEK'S FATHER

But first, surely, we will go and eat together. Let us all enter the palace and be seated.

Butler, is everything ready? As you love me, say that we may go in and dine, my liege accompanied by his lords.
(All go down into the platea.)

THE DUKE'S BUTLER

All is prepared. You direct the seating, Meriasek, and we shall serve the meal. Trumpets and clarions, make music for us now and make it festive.

MERIASEK

My liege lord is to be seated here in the place of highest honor and my father across from him; my dear mother at the end of the table. High-ranking Duke of Orleans,[9] kindly be seated just here, the remaining lords, senior and junior, distributing themselves along both sides of the table.

DUKE OF ORLEANS

Many thanks, courteous Meriasek. The charm of your breeding has won you the affection of many, and your manners are so pleasing to both cleric and layman as to set you apart from all others.
(Here the musicians shall play a tune.)

MERIASEK

Enjoy yourself, my liege; also each and every one of our other guests — dukes, counts, knights. And for you, Father and Mother who nurtured me, the wish of my heart is to see you at your ease.

KING CONAN

We are much obliged to you, gentle Meriasek. Finding you so full

of courtesy, I shall surely make you an important man; to which
end, I know where you will find a wife who is the daughter of an
illustrious king. She will bring you a handsome dowry: manors,
towns, and castles. If it is agreeable to you and your parents, I will
say who she is.

MERIASEK'S FATHER

Much thanks, our good lord. We shall always be grateful to you
for your kind offices; likewise the more firmly established, by
virtue of our son's marriage, and of increased influence.

THE MOTHER

We are gratified and will assuredly be guided by you, as will
Meriasek; else we should be at fault. You are the head of our
family, our royal and most gracious overlord.

MERIASEK

A thousand thanks to you, my liege, for your beneficent inten-
tions in my behalf. But lest I incur your majesty's displeasure,
before this company I beg that you and likewise my father and
mother will excuse me. I do not wish to surrender myself to the
world or ever to marry.

THE FATHER

For my sake, say no more, Meriasek. You shall marry some
worthy lady, dear son. The family will be the stronger through that
marriage and its fruit.

THE MOTHER

If he remained a bachelor, people would laugh at us. Meriasek,
do not talk nonsense. Up to now, you have always been considered
a reasonable child. By all that's decent, keep your good name!

MERIASEK

Let there be no talk of marriage for me — ever. My mind is firmly
fixed on another way of life.

THE FATHER

What other way? Tell me, Meriasek. Oh, the pity of it, my dear boy, if you choose this moment to go mad.

MERIASEK

No, no! Through Christ's grace, I would never want that! My wish, dear father, is to be dubbed a knight of God that I may bear allegiance to Jesus Christ, the mighty one. Such is the order which pleases me, pleases me so greatly that it will be my choice for as long as I live.

KING CONAN

Why must you refuse worldly rank when you are born of noble blood on both your father's and your mother's side? Surely your notions do your family no credit. Give thought to other and better courses, my son.

THE FATHER

Alas, that I ever sent you to school, Meriasek. You have made me regret it. Of any wisdom you may have acquired there, not a trace remains. We shall be the laughing-stock of the whole country. What is to become of the land we own, the towns we possess, our flawless titles to both, if you refuse to marry?

MERIASEK

Father, make Christ your heir or let your property go to the next of kin. Where it may go can never be my concern. I shall never have anything to do with it.

KING CONAN

It seems clear to me, Meriasek, that you are not being any too sensible when you act in opposition to your parents. I don't know what you accomplished at school, but of anything worthwhile you may have learned, there's not a scrap left.

MERIASEK

Christ said: "Whosoever would follow me, let him forsake the ranks of mankind, regardless of degree; the world's lands and dwellings; his father and mother, his friends and relations; and he shall obtain a multitude of gifts and the perfect and everlasting life of the world to come." I will find it for you in Luke's Gospel, his very words as he set them down.[10]

KING CONAN

Why can you not marry here on earth as many a worthy man has done and still been much beloved of God? By the saints in heaven, you have vexed me by thus causing your family to be jeered at and to experience grievous chagrin.

MERIASEK

For the love of Christ on high, I pray that no man will ever know distress or sorrow because of me.

KING CONAN

In all kindness, Meriasek, I ask you to listen to me lest, to put it frankly, you come to regret that you didn't. Ponder this well: your father and I can assuredly convey the land to someone else, if we choose, so that it will never come to you.

You would thus be reduced to beggary while we, as your kinsmen, would bear the blame. The pity of it, were we to be so shamed! Think again before it is too late.

MERIASEK

Were my inheritance to become another man's estate, my high born liege, I should be only too delighted. It would cause me no distress. If I can but have heaven's land, fie on this world and its foul delights!

KING CONAN

I am greatly astonished to witness your scorn of earthly possessions. Neither you nor anyone else can long survive without means. Through wealth and zeal at arms a man moves upward and wins the respect of his lordly peers. Through wealth he enters the ranks of the nobility among those qualified for high station. What does a poor man amount to? However distinguished his ancestry, he remains an inferior, hat in hand. To the moneyed, to the influential, he is an invisible man.

MERIASEK

Do not speak of soldierly enterprise where I am concerned, nor do earthly possessions interest me in the least. Many's the man who has been led astray by riches.

As one may read of Dives,[11] he never lacked for wealth, but what became of his soul? It went to the dread agonies of hell.

Lazarus, now, was a poor man who knew the bitterness of toil. Yet when he died, Abraham received him into the glory and the peace of his bosom.

KING CONAN

(He rises and walks about in the platea.)

Sirs, get yourselves up from the table! I regret that I ever came here. Ah, Meriasek, wretch that you are, do you really suppose that a rich man can never go to heaven? By my soul, I believe you're hopelessly out of your mind, gone mad!

MERIASEK

The Scriptures say that it is fully as hard for a rich man to go to heaven as for a ship's hawser to pass through a needle's eye.

But if the hawser's thickness is reduced to separate strands, the threading can be done. Similarly with a man of wealth. Be diligent, therefore, in giving a portion of your riches to the poor.

KING CONAN

Farewell, knightly Duke. By Christ my maker, your son is mad! Thanks to him, my journey here and the trouble I've gone to have been wasted. The longer I live, upon my soul, the less I'll like him. *(Let Conan exit.)*

THE FATHER

Thank you so much, my lord, for making him such an advantageous offer. What a pity, dear son, that you refuse to be guided by prudence. The sovereign is indeed displeased with you, as are we, your father and mother.

MERIASEK

Although your displeasure is the last thing I would have wanted to incur, I hope that I am in accord with Jesus Christ the merciful. Father and Mother, give me your blessings before I press on my way to learn further the nature of goodness. For the love of the Father, the Son, and the Holy Ghost, do not tempt me into folly.

THE FATHER

My son, I commit you to the hands of God above. I can do no more for you. Make your own way; you have my blessing.

THE MOTHER

Amen to that, and my blessing. Kiss me, my son. How sad I am at this parting!

(Here the Bishop of Cornouaille shall parade.)

BISHOP OF CORNOUAILLE

I am the Bishop of Cornouaille[12] in Brittany, my grace ever bountiful, my peers few anywhere, while in Little Britain there are none to match the worth of my episcopate or its princely rule over the clergy.
(Here Meriasek wears a priest's gown.[13])

MERIASEK

My lord bishop, joy to you. I wish to ask that you confer orders upon me. I seek to become a priest that I may administer the holy sacrament of Christ's body, provided, when you have examined me, my learning is deemed adequate.
(The Bishop of Cornouaille descends into the platea.)

BISHOP OF CORNOUAILLE

Welcome among us, Meriasek. I have heard many good things about you, my dear son. I will grant you orders. By me, forthwith, you shall be ordained in the name of Jesus.
(Meriasek kneels.)
Christ grant that you may ever preserve yourself in purity.

A BLIND MAN

May God bless you, good folk. I am a blind man. Give me your alms, and I will pray for you to Jesus Christ the merciful, savior of all who believe in him.

A CRIPPLED MAN

I also am handicapped. My legs are so twisted by disease that I can scarcely walk. From a full heart I beg you to heal us both.

MERIASEK

(He kneels.)

Jesus, Lord, I beseech you to cure this man who is blind. Jesus Christ, king ever glorious, unfailingly give him his sight. Lord Jesus, full of grace, heal also this cripple. Jesus, Lord, born of a virgin, show your royal power here and now. *In nomine Patris et Filii,* may Christ's virtue, O infirm ones, make you whole!

BLIND MAN

May Christ Jesus reward you, I now see well! I know that in this place your prayers are blessed, your words glorified.

CRIPPLE

And I am wondrously healed, I who have most certainly been a cripple for these many years! I am stricken no more, thanks to Jesus and to this man.

(He ends and moves away on the platea.)

BISHOP OF CORNOUAILLE

We bow the head to you, Meriasek, knowing right well from this moment that our Lord and Savior cherishes you. We beg you to stay with us and be assured that we shall never fail you.

MERIASEK

Many thanks, my lord bishop, but it is my intention to make my way to another country. May the blessing of all the saints ever be upon you and your household.

BISHOP'S CROZIER-BEARER

God bless you, Meriasek! We would be happy to have you remain here with us, yet we ought not to detain you against your will, surely.
(The Bishop of Cornouaille goes up.)

MERIASEK

My blessing, sailors. If you are about to depart for Cornwall, I should like to go with you. I have little to offer for my passage, but I will pray to Christ Jesus that his help may always be yours.

SHIPMASTER

You are welcome to join us, good man. God willing, we will put you ashore on Land's End[14] before the week is out.
(Meriasek goes up into the ship.)
Come right aboard. Men, hoist sail at once.

CREWMAN

There she is, clear to the peak. Now, mate, make fast the halyard....
It's come on to blow a full gale, the sea's gone mad! I see us lost and drowned here, the whole ship's company!

SHIPMASTER

Ah, woe to us that we were ever born! We shall all be lost. Let each man go and make his confession to another, there is nothing else to do. Not one of us will survive. How sad to have come to this!

MERIASEK

Oh, take heart! Christ will aid us. I will pray to him that if such is his wish, no man, whether on land or sea, need be in danger if he calls on Christ and on me.

SHIPMASTER

Meriasek, may your name be honored. Through you we have surely been saved in the hour of peril. Proceed ashore, excellent

man. By Christ's grace, you have reached Cornwall as was your wish.
(Meriasek disembarks in Cornwall.)

MERIASEK

Thanks be to Jesus, I have arrived in a country new to me, which I shall explore. May my precious Lord guide me to a fair spot where I will be able to worship the dear Christ and Mary, flower of maidens.

I have made my way inland and am weary. Mary, Virgin Mother, if you have a house or a shrine near this place, direct me to it, for deep is my desire to make for myself an oratory linked with a house of Mary....

Good man, joy to you. What house is that?

NATIVE

I will tell you. That house is called the Chapel of Mary of Camborne.[15] In return, good fellow, tell me where you're from that you should have to ask.

MERIASEK

As God chose to instruct me, I have come over the sea to this country from Brittany. Here, beside the Chapel of Mary ever blessed, I wish to establish an oratory.[16] Is there water near at hand? No other drink shall ever pass my lips.

NATIVE

Water is very scarce hereabouts. In fact, one has to fetch it from quite some distance. If I could get my hands on ale or wine, I wouldn't often be drinking water, that's for sure. Wouldn't be worth my while, it wouldn't.

MERIASEK

I am minded to look about me to the north and east of the chapel in search of water for my use.
(Let him go over to the meadow. He kneels.)
Lord Jesus, I beseech you to grant my prayer for water as once in

the long ago, by your grace, you gave it from the hard rock to Moses.
(Here water springs up in the well.)[17]

NATIVE

Good sir, bless you for bringing us water for our comfort and convenience. What's happened here surely proves that God loves you.

A FEVER-SUFFERER

O God, what shall I do? Alas, I have a consuming disease men call the ague. I've had daily attacks of it for several months. My very vitals are weakened from the pain.

A CRIPPLE

I am completely crippled. God, how thankful I'd be if I could die and leave this world. They say there's a man at Camborne[18] who performs miracles with ease. We ought to hurry to him there and beg him wholeheartedly to cure us.
(Let them go over to Meriasek.)

FEVER-SUFFERER

Joy to you, Meriasek. We are a pair of unfortunates. I am fever-ridden, while this man is totally crippled. Neither of us can earn so much as a bare living, and that's the truth. For the love of Christ, cure us!

MERIASEK

(He kneels.)
May Jesus, lord of heaven and earth, grant you healing. Jesus, Lord, I beseech you to restore these men to health. Mary, mother full of grace, intercede for them with thy Son Our Lord. Mary, Virgin Mother, assist me with your prayers. Rise up, good men, and tell me how it is with you now.

CRIPPLE

Glory to Christ, I am whole again, body and limbs! I can walk — with ease!

FEVER-SUFFERER

I too am cured, thanks be to Christ! Noble Meriasek, filled with holy power and favored of God, we are bound to honor him outright, no matter the risk.

MERIASEK

Give thanks to Christ and not to me, good men....It is here and now, the merciful Christ willing, that I shall choose a site and later found a church[19] for the perpetual worship of Christ; here, in accordance with my purpose, close by holy Mary's chapel.

A DISEASED MAN

Alas, alas, what am I to do? A loathsome disease has invaded my face. No man can endure me. I have learned there is a great healer in Camborne. I will go to see whether he can cure me....
(To Meriasek)
Good cheer to you, Meriasek. For the sake of Christ, I beg you to help me, a wretched man. My face is so diseased that few people can bring themselves to look at me.

MERIASEK

(He kneels.)
May the God of heaven, who in former days freed Naaman[20] from his leprosy, free you. I will cleanse you with water. If the hour of your deliverance has come, may Jesus Christ, God of mercy, succor you.

NATIVE

For a certainty, you are beautifully healed, thanks to gentle Meriasek who is, as all of us can see, full of grace and beloved of God.

DISEASED MAN

I am deeply grateful to you, Meriasek. May Christ in the fullness of his grace and the Virgin Mary in her glory reward you on high. By the Lord, how great must be the number of the infirm you have healed here below!

36

(Let them go off, Meriasek waiting at Camborne.)

(Here Teudar shall parade.)

TEUDAR

Teudar[21] by name, I am the reigning lord in Cornwall. That Mohammed be honored in these parts, near and far, is my unceasing command. Severe torture and a cruel death await the worshippers of any other god.[22]

MESSENGER

Hail, Lord Teudar! I bear news, but I simply haven't the courage to give it to you aloud. No, I don't dare. As I have good reason to know, upon my soul, it wouldn't be to my advantage.

TEUDAR

What the devil has happened? Let's have it, you oaf. Ay, speak, you rascally twister. Damnation, can't the filth hear me? Just speak, dead ears! Speak, ruin seize your throat. Ay, say something! You son of perdition, the devil take you!

MESSENGER

In Penwith a little west of Carn Brea,[23] there's a priest at work curing the blind, the deaf, and the crippled, besides every other ailment under the sun. He won't stand for the mention of any god except Christ, who was put to death and then, he says, was brought back to life again.

TEUDAR

Out, woe's me for sheer trouble! What devil's hole am I in now? Out, woe's me that I wasn't dead before I was born. Woe! For shame! Soldiers, let's be on our way to settle with this priest in the devil's name!

FIRST SOLDIER

My lord, we will accompany you. I first heard of the man months ago. He gives the blind their sight and enables the deaf to hear.

37

SECOND SOLDIER

I tell you, Teudar, the country is making much of this fellow. If he isn't taken down a peg, the people won't rate Mohammed any higher than they would a dog.

TEUDAR

(He goes down.)
Let us set out in force, my knights, and let me be informed without delay where the priest is living....

MESSENGER

I'm sure I see him, royal lord, yonder on the flat. He's got to be coming from the chapel....

TEUDAR

You there, young man, turn this way! I want you to tell me your name, lineage, and religion and be quick about it.

MERIASEK

I am Meriasek, a descendant of the Conan line. I believe in Christ Jesus, the beloved. I believe that he is very God, born of Mary, both virgin and mother. That is my faith.

TEUDAR

You come from good stock, Meriasek, and should think twice before disgracing yourself. Don't talk about a thing for which there is no visible proof, I say. It is entirely contrary to reason, believe me, that without male seed a woman can conceive a child.

MERIASEK

You are failing to comprehend the higher law which of necessity applies to the birth of Jesus Christ into the world and to his treasured Passion. Even as the sun's light passes through glass without rupturing it, a thing you have seen for yourself, so Christ from on high entered Mary's womb without tainting her flesh in the least. Jesus was conceived, indeed, by the power of the most precious Holy Spirit.

TEUDAR

Don't attempt to bamboozle me. Though you were to go on running off at the mouth forever, Jesus had to have a father as well as a mother. Out of all you've said, not one blasted word is true.

MERIASEK

If you were able to understand, you would realize that God on high was his father. To redeem Adam and his posterity, Jesus took it upon himself to enter this world, where he experienced an agonizing death. He freed the souls of men from bondage to Satan and brought them to bliss.

TEUDAR

I tell you, Meriasek, had God on high really been his father, Jesus could have saved everyone by the power of his grace without having to die at all. Your claim is ridiculous. Where was the need for the Son of God to be butchered like a stag?

MERIASEK

Because Adam, our parent, sinned, both he and his descendants were condemned to hell. But the Godhead willed that he should be redeemed unto salvation. The Son was begotten and took flesh upon him inasmuch as it was not fitting that the Godhead undergo the Passion.

TEUDAR

This argument will gain us nothing were we to carry on with it here for all eternity. Meriasek, reject Christ and I will become your friend for all to see. I'll make you an honored bishop, chief prelate over the length and breadth of the country. The only thing I ask is that you worship Mohammed from this day forward.

MERIASEK

There is a better way. It is for you to worship the beloved Christ, else you are surely lost.

TEUDAR

Speak no more of Christ, not a word! If you do, I'll make you sorry for it. Listen to me before it's too late and come to your senses, for if once I let myself go, the devil himself will rise from hell before I let up. And that's the truth of it.

By my soul, I am reluctant to harm you, my dear Meriasek, provided you reverence my gods in their beauty.

MERIASEK

Fie on your gods, three thousand times over! Surely they are all devils. I will never bend the knee to them, and do not look to me for anything whatever of that kind. If you want to do something useful in the world, reject them. You are a fool to trust in them.

TEUDAR

Out upon you, you lying word-juggler, who dares to flout my sublime gods! Regardless of prince or emperor, you shall hang for the fool you are. Every day that passes I'll despise you more, you, a renegade from your own country. Say a word against my dignity and you'll bitterly regret it.

I am emperor here and governor, conqueror of territory, a worthy and very powerful lord. Look about you and see!

MERIASEK

Pray be silent and hold your blathering tongue. You waste much breath. In all seriousness, you would do better to become a Christian, worshipping Christ in fullness of heart. I will baptize you forthwith.

TEUDAR

Out, woe's me! Make way for me to remove myself from here as quickly as possible. It's the devil himself who confronts me, wanting to baptize me! I'm as good as dead on the spot if I stay here another instant. Take vengeance, Mohammed, on this disturber of my peace!
(*He ascends.*)

Torturers, come here! Torturers, if you are loyal, torturers, come to me at once! Ai, ai, ai! You aren't paying attention.
(*He descends.*)

They've got to be fetched since all my distress produces no result.
(Here sticks ready for Teudar and his men.)

Ho, there, ho! Where are you fellows? I'll baste your confounded skulls. What's going on? Taking a nap, are you? Ho, can't you hear me calling? That's right, have a bite to eat before you're up and doing.

Fall to it! Start thrashing!
(And they beat them.)

FIRST TORTURER

My lord, my lord, don't beat us any more! Tell us what you want done and we'll surely do it.

TEUDAR

Go to Camborne, to the west of Carn Brea. There you're certain to find a bold upstart who goes by the name of Meriasek, a son of the Fiend. He's a Christian. Seize him, put him to the torture — see that you're not slack about it — and if he won't deny his Christ, pay the whoreson back double for his stubbornness. If you happen to kill him, I'll back you up, never fear.

SECOND TORTURER

We'll do it, my lord. Let's be off at once, each keeping a sharp lookout in a different direction. As for me, on my soul I'll show you the quickest way to Camborne.
(Teudar departs to his station.)

MERIASEK

Thanks be to God! A vision has warned me that I should leave this country at once and return to Brittany, thus evading the false Teudar. His plot against me shall fail.

On this place which I have founded, here beside Mary of Camborne, may Christ Jesus ever bestow his grace. May the Trinity and Mary the Virgin always be held in honor here, and may the seven sacraments, whether on days of feasting or of labor, ever be administered in time to come.

If a faithful Christian shall be seized by tertian fever and at this spot remember me, Jesus, precious Lord, cure him of his affliction.

I pray likewise that the water from my well may be a remedy for the man who has lost his wits, bringing him back again to sanity.[24] Jesus, Lord of Salvation, grant this through thy merciful kindness.

To this place I give my blessing. In a little while I must depart, for my enemies draw near. Meantime, keeping to open country, I shall rest here beneath this rock.[25]

(Here Meriasek shall conceal himself under the rock.)

SECOND TORTURER

Have you spied Meriasek? That keen-eyed fellow isn't anywhere in Camborne, the devil take him!

THIRD TORTURER

No more suppers for you. He's made off into open country. His own mother's curse on him!

MENIAL

We could give the brush and the rock a once-over in case he's hiding. But, oh well, let's just leave him be. He's not going to be found. I say go home.

FIRST TORTURER

What devil's hole can he have gone to? Teudar will go mad when he hears the man's gotten away.

SECOND TORTURER

That's his problem. Why didn't he grab him while they were jawing each other?

THIRD TORTURER

(To Teudar)

Hail, Teudar, in your castle. Meriasek has simply vanished from these parts. We haven't an idea how. In towns and on downs we've searched for him, and that's a fact. Nobody is able to offer a word as to his whereabouts.

TEUDAR

Out! Help, help! Oh, woe, to think that he has gotten away. Not for a double share in the wealth of all the world would I want that to happen. No, not that, I wouldn't! Oh, you muddle-heads. For the rest of my days it's 'out upon you,' you hopeless rascals!

MENIAL

Look here, Teudar. Take it easy, confound you! Why didn't you keep him while you had him and were talking with him? Not to chop things too fine, his God is unwilling to see him harmed. *(Teudar goes down.)*

TEUDAR

Is this all the comfort I'm to get from you? Truly, sirs, when I suffer it gives you pleasure. Well, no matter. Before we part, by glorious Apollyon,[26] only some of you will feel like laughing. I'm going to even things with the Hobbyhorse and his companions.[27] Take that, you four loafers! and next time remember better what I order you to do.
(He beats them.)

MERIASEK

Thanks be to Jesus, I have had rest indeed under the shelter of this rock. My enemies have gone away. It was God's will that they could not capture me. In future this shall be known as Meriasek's Rock.

I will make my way toward the sea and there seek ship's passage.... God's blessing on you, worthy captain, may he guard your vessel from harm. If you are headed for Brittany, I beg to be allowed to go with you.

SHIPMASTER

You seem an honest man. Join us aboard, therefore, in God's name. Hoist sail, mate. We have a fair wind.... The Coast of Brittany is in plain sight.

CREWMAN

The Channel is safely crossed. Faith, it's been a good run, we've made land. You're free to go ashore whenever you like, Meriasek. *(He disembarks.)*

See, the very rocks have bowed their welcome to you on shore, thanks to the might of Jesus.

MERIASEK

May God reward you, good men, and may the Lord Jesus, full of grace, guide my steps aright. If I go to my family, they'll tempt me toward worldliness.

A BRETON

Good sir, take care which way you go. Along that road there's a huge wolf. If you chance to meet up with it, it will bloody you. Oh me, look there! There it is!

MERIASEK

Beast, I command you never to harm me or any other Christian from this time forward. Don't be afraid, good man. See how tame it is, letting me stroke it. It's willing to follow me without thought of attack.

BRETON

You must surely be a holy man. That creature has been a constant killer of men, women, and children throughout the countryside, yet look at it now, following you as meek as a lamb. We are very greatly beholden to you.

MERIASEK

It has not attempted to do injury to me nor shall it receive injury from me or anyone else. In the name of Christ, the Virgin's Son, I command you, beast, to go into the wilderness and leave human beings alone from this day forward. In Jesus' name, go your separate way.

I, too, will betake me into the wild, there to live as a true hermit, worshipping my God in freedom from worldly enticements for the rest of my life....

Yes, here, not far from Castle Pontivy, on the summit of this mount above the river Josselin,[28] I shall build a chapel dedicated to the service of Blessed Mary, even though the spot be desolate and cold.

(He ascends the mountain.)

Glory to Christ, the Maiden's Son! Though the mountain must surely measure a thousand paces from its base to its summit,[29] God will help me. This is where I will establish my oratory, laying the foundations forthwith.

(A chapel ready. Here Meriasek wears a russet mantle and a beard.)

HERE BEGINS THE EPISODE OF
ST. SILVESTER (Part I)[30]

(Constantine shall here parade, saying:)

CONSTANTINE

By virtue of my unique distinction among men and the awe in which I am held by the people, I am known as Constantine the Great,[31] an emperor of unquestioned worth, scion of Queen Helena, leader of all my tribe, my status widely acknowledged.

There exists in this kingdom at present a false religion, provoking me to such devilish anger that if I am destined to live even a little longer, I am resolved to suppress these cultists. By my soul I swear it! In abysmal pain and disgrace, they shall all perish at my hand. Having already slain hundreds, I propose to slay further hundreds. Executioners, my madcaps all, come to me, in the name of Mohammed and Sol![32]

(Here the executioners shall parade armed with swords.)

EXECUTIONERS

Hail, Constantine the Mighty! As your loyal subjects, we assemble to do you honor and for your glory. Your enemies, if we find them, will never laugh again.

45

CONSTANTINE

Welcome, knights every one! Your mission is to take to the road and punish every Christian to be found anywhere in the kingdom of Rome. Torture to death all who believe in Mary's Son, and have no fear of condemnation. I shall always defend you.

SECOND EXECUTIONER

We fear neither the risk nor the sin. My arms have been so long on holiday from killing Christians, they itch. Assign us a complement of soldiers who like action.

CONSTANTINE

You shall have two hundred of them to accompany you. See that you conduct yourselves like men when it comes to letting Christian blood. Spare neither the young nor the old among the enemies of our god, Sol.

THIRD EXECUTIONER

Be assured, we will not, Constantine. Piercing agonies await all who worship Christ, that beggar. Let's be on our way at once, comrades, and let each knight keep sharp lookout along his own route for any straying traitor.

MENIAL

I see a couple of men over yonder. By the looks of them, they could be Christians. Sirs, on pain of death, tell us here and now what religion you follow.

COUNT

We believe in Jesus, the Christ. No man on earth can frighten us into forsaking that name. Whoever does not believe on it will surely go down to hell when he dies and to hell's torment.

FIRST EXECUTIONER

Away with you, you dirty dog! Never mention Christ in our presence, for if you do, you'll die, since it is Constantine himself

46

who has sent us into these parts for the sole purpose of destroying Christians.

DOCTOR OF SACRED STUDIES

Despite dread Constantine or fear of torture, we will not deny Jesus. If you maltreat us, Christ, who is Lord of Lords, will avenge us.

SECOND EXECUTIONER

Don't you threaten us, you son of a whore! Fie on you and on your Christ a thousand times over!
(The gallows ready.)
Deny his name this instant and call on Jove and Sol, or else you'll die in torture on this very spot.

COUNT

We would rather die than worship a devil in this world of clay.[33] Ah, God, how foolish you are that you will not turn to Christ, who in his mercy suffered death for all mankind.

THIRD EXECUTIONER

For such vile talk, you shall be hanged, hanged right here, and I'm going to string up this other traitor close beside you; two villains shoulder to shoulder.

DOCTOR OF SACRED STUDIES

Mary, Queen of Heaven, pray for us and for our salvation. And you, accursed men, take heed for your souls in peril of damnation. *(He ends.)*

MENIAL

Hold your tongue! Leave it to me to save myself. When have you seen an unclaimed soul in this world? Though heaven's gates are shut, hell still gapes wide. Which way I go is all one to me.

COUNT

Jesus, precious Lord, grant us salvation, for now we must die.

May the time be blessed! Jesus, unto you I entrust my spirit.
(He ends.)

FIRST EXECUTIONER

Now that their necks are stretched, let's add to their discomfort. Let's skewer them on our swords, in one side and out the other. That way the devil can peel them. Look, this one is done for.

SECOND EXECUTIONER

I'll do the same for the other, seeing I don't like to just stand around. There she goes...clean through the tripes. Next, I'll lay open his skull so his brains can ooze away drop by drop.

THIRD EXECUTIONER

We're always ready to do the devil's work. Hang anybody who isn't. Look at those two who have fallen into the dust. They're one mass of wounds like a badger torn by a hound.[34]

MENIAL[35]

Wicked men like you never fail to boast the loudest over their worst crimes, but your luck will turn. I leave with you this farewell: May God damn you all!
(Let the Menial go off and the Executioners wait in the platea.)

JESUS

(In heaven)
My angels, white as crystal, speed the martyred souls to their reward. By their suffering on earth, they have gained the joy that endures forever.

MICHAEL

Lord Jesus, your will be done. Those who are martyred on earth shall ascend to perfect happiness in heaven. As it should be, your command shall ever be faithfully obeyed.

GABRIEL

O martyred souls, heaven's bliss is yours through the grace of Jesus Christ on high. Because of the agony you have endured in the

flesh here below, your spirits shall have joy everlasting.
(Here the souls ready.)

FIRST EXECUTIONER

Out! Let's get out of here, comrades! Which way doesn't matter as long as we find cover or else we'll all be burned. Very close, I swear, there fell a brightness so like lightning that it made me start.

(Here St. Silvester[36] begins, saying:)

SILVESTER

In the name and to the glory of God, who created heaven and earth and with his hands did shape mankind from clay, grant unto us, who are meek and lowly of heart, thy peace. The Father, the Son, and the Holy Ghost, three Persons and one Substance, that is the true faith as taught by Holy Church.

And now, my children, we shall go hence together in order that we may bury the good men who, I hear, have been martyred by wicked men. That Emperor Constantine's representatives will not spare the life of a single Christian in this land seems quite certain....
(He descends. The tomb ready.)

A CARDINAL

Silvester, our dear Father, may the might of Jesus Christ Our Lord ever aid us. Here are the martyrs' bodies. Let us bury them at once and depart without delay.
(Here they bury the bodies.)

SILVESTER

Now that they are in the grave, Lord Jesus Christ, king of the angelic host, preserve their souls. As for us, we will withdraw for the time being to see whether, at least for the present, we can protect ourselves from Constantine. If not, he will kill us.

We shall go to Mt. Soracte[37] since we ought not to remain longer in Rome. Come away with me now, all my clergy of whatever rank, and let us see if we can protect ourselves for a season....

(He goes up to Mt. Soracte.)

(A mask ready upon Constantine's face.)

SECOND EXECUTIONER

Hail, Constantine, sire and lord! We have exterminated more than sixty Christians: some hanged, some beheaded, some dragged behind horses, some burnt to ashes.
(Let him go off.)

CONSTANTINE

Return to your homes, my soldiers, and may the devil watch over you. For my part, alas, I am stricken with leprosy[38] and cannot account for it. On every tongue the word for me, the leper, is hideous. Everyone loathes the sight of my face.

Ah, wretched that I am, what's to be done for me now? My persecution of the Christians has been excessive in its cruelty. I acknowledge that. Pleasure, riches, oh, farewell! For me the world holds so little joy, I want to die, here and now, no longer to be seen among men.

A JUSTICE

Send for the bishops and the eminent doctors. If there is anywhere in the world a cure for the disease, they will spell it out from books, for they are great readers of the stars. Therefore, have no fear in the matter. They will give you relief.

CONSTANTINE

Messenger, make haste to fetch the bishop here to me and the illustrious doctor as well, he who is called the most learned man alive. Let us see whether they can tell me that a sure cure exists for my affliction.

MESSENGER[39]

Hail, Emperor Constantine! Here I am, prepared to travel far, far from home on an errand of yours, nor will I drag my feet. I will

50

bring the bishop and the peerless doctor to your palace, proceeding at a fast trot....

(Here the Bishop of Poli[40] or the Doctor shall parade.)

MESSENGER

Hail, my lord bishop, in your tower, and hail to you as well, Doctor! What luck to find you both in the same place! Constantine has need of your presence, and it would be advisable to look carefully before you leap, as it will be crucial to come up with wise answers.

BISHOP OF POLI

You are most heartily welcome here, Messenger, upon my soul! But what ails Constantine? Can it be that he is not in good health, eh? Enlighten us. If he is ill, we shall assuredly find a means of making him well again.

DOCTOR

Sick! Here's a chance to strike a healthy bargain.[41] Be so good as to inform me, dear messenger, what seems to be the matter with our comely emperor.

MESSENGER

Frankly, he has become a segregated leper. I doubt that I've ever seen anyone in a worse state than he.

DOCTOR

Aha! I knew it, I knew it! Apprentice Jenkin, be so good as to lay hold of my book of physic. Carry it under your arm and see to it that you build me up as a physician who knows his business.
(An earthen pot, the book ready, and the urinal to be inspected.)[42]

APPRENTICE JENKIN

When it comes to easing the bowels and controlling a tertian fever,[43] your luck is good. And if you happen to find yourself thigh to thigh with some girl, you'd prove you knew that kind of business too.

BISHOP OF POLI

Glory to the Throne and joy to you, Lord of the Kingdom! We have come to you at once, accompanied by your messenger.

CONSTANTINE

Welcome, eminent bishop. Welcome to you likewise, worthy doctor. Come up, please. You can observe my leprosy at a glance. It is by no means a merely latent condition. Can you cure me?

DOCTOR

I wish first to examine the urine, and then the emperor shall have an answer to his question.

JUSTICE

I foresaw that need. Here is the specimen. Pour it into your blue glass container.

DOCTOR

Hoc urinum malorum, it's diseased, *et nimis rubrorum,* and too red. Ah, I know the condition well. Come here, young Jenkin. Look up, raise your head. Hey, look up, confound you!

Don't be squeamish just because it stinks to high heaven. Put your nose up close. This is a ticklish matter, but I'm now certain of my diagnosis.

What will you give me, Constantine, if I cure you? With the help of my god, Sol,[44] I will prepare a medicinal draught for you, provided I get the necessary cash to buy the ingredients.

CONSTANTINE

Here, take these ten pounds. Accept them as a payment on account. Make me well again, and you will find yourself better off for life. I shall raise you to high religious office.

DOCTOR

Strike me blue, these will come in handy! I beg leave to go home

at this time. On Thursday I shall return with a potion that ought to heal you.
(Here he goes down with his apprentice. The Bishop of Poli remains where he is.)

Faith, I can't refuse to give it a try, not when, by Sol, a handsomer fee hasn't come my way in ages. But what the devil do I know about how to cure your disease, Constantine? After all, though, one must live. If fakery doesn't work, a physician will never get ahead. *(Let him go home.)*

APPRENTICE

If a doctor has any better remedies than his lies, I swear I don't know what in the world they are.
(Let him go home.)

CONSTANTINE

What is your opinion, bishop? For my part, I am not convinced that an effective cure for my condition is obtainable from books.

BISHOP OF POLI

No, my liege, it is not. I give you my word. I have been reading up on the subject for the past three months. You will never be restored to health unless and until you are washed in blood.

PRELATE

We have indeed been looking into the matter. If you were bathed in pure blood you would be completely restored and in no other way. The books tell us that much.

CONSTANTINE

What kind of blood is required? You are not to spare any animal in existence, if obtainable, since otherwise, as you can see for yourselves, I would remain in want of a cure.

BISHOP OF POLI

Animal blood is useless. You must collect children from everywhere in the country, more particularly infants at the breast. The pure blood of children is a supreme remedy. Immerse yourself

53

in that and you will return to health.

PRELATE

Send soldiers into the region to assemble, yes, as many as three thousand children. Have them butchered and their pure blood collected in a clean vat. Once you have bathed in it, your flesh will become as flawless as crystal.

CONSTANTINE

This is a feasible project. Executioners, forthwith. Executioners, come quick. Executioners, at full power! Executioners, wake up!

FIRST EXECUTIONER[45]

Hail, my lord Constantine! Here we are, peasant and gentleman alike, not that I suppose you have summoned us for an exercise in good works. That has never been your style.

CONSTANTINE

You are to go out and cover for me the entire country, Lombardy[46] as well as Rome, and round up children under the age of four. Have three thousand of them come here, together with their mothers. An extra hundred won't matter. Let each of you proceed to his own district. A force of armed men will be divided among you. Whoever supplies the largest number of children will receive the most thanks, yes, and a maximum bounty.
(Men-at-arms ready.)

SECOND EXECUTIONER

Lord, your commands shall be obeyed. A quarter of the assembled force will follow me....

You, woman with a small child, march yourself off to the Emperor Constantine at speed and take your brood-mare neighbor with you, or I'll slaughter you where you stand.

THIRD EXECUTIONER

I've now got together a hundred and twenty brats. Off with them to the Emperor so they can be bled like pigs or calves. Soldiers, see to it that not one woman escapes.

MENIAL

By my soul, I've collected a hundred and sixty chicks. That's enough for my share. It's put the mothers in a proper flap, but when these are gone, we'll just make more....

FIRST EXECUTIONER

(To Constantine in the presence of the women and children.)

Hail, Constantine, in your tower! I have been hard at work all over the country in order to fulfill your wishes. Here are nineteen hundred children. Hearts are sure to break at the sight of their slaughter.

SECOND EXECUTIONER

I have returned, Constantine, bringing with me at least six hundred children. I stand ready to let their blood. Behold the tender crop!

THIRD EXECUTIONER

Hail, Constantine the Noble! I have borne many a curse for the sake of pleasing you. A plague on any child who has escaped, plus some whose hearts have given out. But my tally is a sure eight hundred. Let them be bled immediately.

MENIAL

Hail, Constantine, in your tower! Out of respect for you, my total exceeds one thousand, one hundred. Moreover, since I set out from home, I have begotten children, I may say, to offset any shrinkage.

FIRST MOTHER

Alas, cruel Emperor, if you intend to murder these sinless little ones, your scheme is infamous! Oh, may the God of Heaven bring down vengeance upon you, you wicked men!

JUSTICE

Do not indulge in empty threats. In truth, these children must die so that our peerless Emperor may have their blood in which to bathe and be restored to beauty without spot. Our learned men have discovered that by this means he can be healed.

CONSTANTINE

What is the sum total of the children who have been procured for me here? The necessity of their death is indeed harrowing. The sight of their weeping mothers moves me to pity, yet, at the same time, I yearn to regain a healthy body.

FIRST EXECUTIONER

To my personal knowledge, there are three thousand children here, actually, three thousand, one hundred and forty. I say kill them, sparing none, for then you can be thoroughly washed in blood. I will kill them for you, indeed, with no more conscience than for an equal number of woodland deer.

SECOND EXECUTIONER

I am prepared to cut the throats of a thousand and bleed them. We shall pile the carcasses and shovel them under in the devil's name. To my way of thinking, there is no more to killing a child than to butchering a goat or a buck. The question of shame is irrelevant.

CONSTANTINE

In Rome, the moral obligations of the blood royal are quite explicit. The law reads: "Whoever takes the life of a child in battle shall be held guilty of a cruel act."[47] Heed my words. I am loath to sacrifice the lives of these children without due cause, nor am I certain that torment does not await my soul after death.

THIRD EXECUTIONER

Emperor and Sire, permit the children to be killed in order that you may now be restored to health. If God will not claim you hereafter, the devil will most gladly do so. If you would ever be whole again, you must wash yourself in the blood of these children. We will kill them as quickly as one snaps his fingers.

MENIAL

So we kill these small fry, girl and boy. What's the loss? In one night, if I do say so myself, I'd start you nine more exactly like this one. If you wish it, sovereign lord, I'll cut its throat and bleed it right here. Zip!

CONSTANTINE

Ah, tender darlings of your mothers, it would be an outrage were you to perish for my sake. We all know what a pitiful thing it would be to sacrifice three thousand young lives to the health of one man.

I would rather die of leprosy and thus preserve the lives of the thousands of little children here than cause so ruthless a slaughter. I should indeed be cruel were I to snuff out all these lives.

On pain of hanging and drawing, give back the children to their mothers. I decree that not a single child shall be killed. Moreover, give the women money to buy something to eat and drink and to furnish the children with good clothing. Return at once to your homes, nursing mothers, you and your little ones.

SECOND MOTHER

Sire, we poor women thank you many times over for the mercy you have shown us. Because you have saved our children, may God give you health, mighty lord!

CONSTANTINE

The night has come, and I will go to my bed, weary of the life that is now mine. If only I might recover my health, I would give half my realm and all my worldly goods....
(He shuts the door.)

JESUS[48]

Peter and Paul, go down to earth and to Constantine. Because he has taken pity on innocent little children, Silvester shall restore him to health.

PETER

Lord, your will be done. Let us go, Brother Paul, to bring comfort to Constantine. Inasmuch as he has refrained from shedding the blood of children, he shall surely be healed.

57

(Peter and Paul go down and ascend into Constantine's tower.)

PAUL

Constantine, if you are asleep, listen with a sleeper's ear to us whose mission is one of healing. Because you showed mercy toward babes and sucklings, Jesus will heal you.

PETER

Because you have withheld your hand from the slaughter of the innocent, Christ has sent us to give you this message: in order to regain perfect health, send word to Silvester to come and make you well.

PAUL

The Holy Father Silvester, presently to be found on Mt. Soracte, will speedily cleanse you from all disease without the sacrifice of a single child.

PETER

And when you have been fully restored to health, take measures to level with the ground all temples dedicated to false gods. In their stead, raise up, support, and maintain as many churches for Jesus Christ as lies within your power.
(Let them pass to heaven.)

CONSTANTINE

Benedicite, what a vision I had during the night! Though the doors were shut tight, two radiant beings came to me and said to send for Silvester and I should unfailingly be cured of all trace of my leprosy.

Messenger, make haste to fetch Silvester to me as quickly as possible. He and his clergy are hiding on Mt. Soracte. Direct them to come to me here in Rome.

MESSENGER

As always, Lord Constantine, I shall promptly obey your orders. Knights, let us be going although, to tell the truth, I don't rightly

know where this Mt. Soracte is located....
(To Silvester on Mt. Soracte.)

Greetings, Silvester and attendant clergy. You are not to remain longer in hiding here.
(The images of Peter and Paul ready with Silvester.)

You are urgently required to present yourselves before the Emperor. He so commands.

SILVESTER

Glory be to God on high! I perceive, brethren, that we must die, a call which may never be evaded. Let us go to meet our fate with one accord, and may Jesus, Son of Salvation, ever sustain us....
(To Constantine)

Hail, Constantine, in your tower! I am aware that you are expecting from us the customary honors, and if your religion were sound, we would have offered them. But in view of your unbelief and despite the threat of death, I will not bow down to you.
(He goes up.)

CONSTANTINE

Silvester, I welcome you. You have not been brought to me in order that I may harm or reproach you. It is rather that I suffer day and night from a grave disease. My learned men, persons of much wisdom, have advised me to take the lives of several thousand innocent young children with the object of bathing myself in their still warm blood.

Three thousand were assembed to that end. Yet it seemed to me a very great pity to sacrifice so many young lives for the sake of one man. I ordered them spared and sent home. But in the night while I lay awake, I had a strange vision. Although the doors were shut, two men appeared before me, surrounded by brilliant light. As I hope to be loved, I have no idea as to their identity.

They made it clear that I should send for Silvester at once, saying: "Before he takes leave of you, he will wash you clean, that your leprosy may be healed." Who were these beings? Can you enlighten me, Silvester? It is my belief they were gods.

SILVESTER

I say they were not gods, Constantine. They were two of the dear Christ's Apostles. Look at these images of them and see if they don't resemble their originals, whose names I will divulge to you.

CONSTANTINE

By my soul, the likenesses are exact. The one with the keys and his companion with a sword, they were the pair who came to me in the night. I swear I have never seen anything more beautiful in my life! Calling upon Christ's mercy, I am firmly resolved to become a Christian.

SILVESTER

I will place you under instruction, and you must faithfully observe a week of penance. After that has been accomplished, you shall be baptized and washed clean so that you may be healed.

CONSTANTINE

It is my earnest desire to do penance, beseeching Christ to have mercy on my sins. In atonement, I will give alms to the poor and the bereaved....

SILVESTER

(He goes down. Holy water ready.)
In the name of Mary's Son, I baptize you. Behold, you are washed clean of sin. I pray that He who died upon the Cross will now grant you perfect healing.
(The mask removed.)[49]

JESUS

For the pity you took on the children, Constantine, and the mercy you showed by refusing to have them killed, I will heal your body now that your soul is cleansed of sin. The merciful shall unfailingly obtain mercy.
(The procession ready.)

CONSTANTINE

Benedicite, how great the light which so lately surrounded me!

60

Past doubt I have seen Christ, the Prince of Healing, all his wounds agape before me. I saw them every one and was divinely comforted.

SILVESTER

You have much reason to rejoice. You were a leper, but thanks be to Christ you are restored to health. Never before in all your life, as far as I know, have you been a handsomer or a more wholesome man.

CONSTANTINE

To Christ Jesus I shall ever give thanks, and to you also, Silvester. Let us go together in procession to your palace. Throughout my kingdom, no god shall be worshipped save Christ, and as long as I live I shall propagate the faith of Jesus and his law.
(To the Pope's palace in procession and afterwards let him go home.)

LIFE OF MERIASEK (Part II)[50]

(Outlaws shall parade here or one for all.)[51]

FIRST OUTLAW

I am a forest outlaw. Never in my life have I been sitting prettier. Whenever the booty gives out, I just get me more. Plundering is the name of the game.

SECOND OUTLAW

It's high time we lined up another job. Faith, chief, we haven't a penny left between the lot of us! Let's put the eye on somebody with a hefty purse, a churchman if we can manage it. They're the kind who'll soon lay their hands on more.

FIRST OUTLAW

On your feet, men. Let's get moving. Keep your eyes peeled for a wandering merchant type and don't think twice about grabbing him. I'll scout ahead and be ready to back you up.
(He goes down.)

61

THIRD OUTLAW

There's a man on horseback, and I'm not holding off any longer.
Here's where I nab him. Whoa! Got you!

Get down, mate, and let's have your purse right out from over
your heart. I'm taking the horse, too.

MERCHANT

Oh, sirs, listen to me! Think of what will happen to your souls
when you die. They will surely pay a price for this in wretchedness
and great pain. Ah, God, woe betide your souls!
(The priest ready.)

FIRST OUTLAW

When did you ever see a human soul left out in the cold in this
world, repenting its sins?

If God won't take me when I die, then it's a sure thing the devil
will and with pleasure, as quick and gay as a hawk.

FOURTH OUTLAW

I spot a lad in a long gown. Nine to one he's a priest, which means
he's going to have money on him. Mister Parson, sir, *bona dies.*
Faith and I'd like to swap purses with you before we part.

PRIEST

Ah, my son, think of your God! Such a deed as this is never in
accordance with his will, never. Reflect on this: you are most
certainly breaking one of God's commandments.

FIRST OUTLAW

Show me a man who's afraid of God, and I'll show you a man who
won't ever get on in the world. Don't be stubborn, mate. Just hand
over all the money you have on you or else I'll chop you here and
now into four pieces.

PRIEST

You have robbed me of all I have, but there will come a time
when Christ Jesus will balance the account between you and me.

Bear this in mind: come the Day of Judgment, you shall infallibly repay me.

FIRST OUTLAW

So you're giving me until Judgment Day to settle, are you? Well, then, since that won't come in the body, for the present you're going to lose everything except your body. Strip him! He's given us quite generous terms, you know — until Doomsday, no less! Repayment won't come any sooner, either.

SECOND OUTLAW

Look at him, he's stark naked! That's the way to cater for the rich lads.
(They wait in the platea.)

(Here the Count of Rohan.)

COUNT OF ROHAN

I am the lord of Rohan, a respected and peerless count. As for Meriasek, a very close relation of mine,[52] he has gone away and broken off contact with his parents. It troubles me that I have no idea of his whereabouts.

FIRST MESSENGER

Sir Count, powerful lord, the news is that Meriasek has returned to this region. He is living the life of a hermit not far from Pontivy.[53]

COUNT OF ROHAN

I and his other kinsmen will go to him to learn whether we can prevail upon him to resume his former estate. His nearest of kin are indeed disturbed about him.

A KINSMAN (Mother's Side)

As I hear it, he has established himself on very high ground at least half a mile up from the valley below. There, completely alone, he spends his nights and days, with little food and no amenities.

(The count goes down toward the mountain with Meriasek's maternal and paternal kin.)

MERIASEK

Here, thanks be to Jesus, I am enabled to live in the wilderness as a hermit. Instead of my former purple silks and other fine fabrics, I now wear coarse gray and under it, next to my skin, a hair shirt.

I drink neither cider nor wine, nor anything else except pure water. I dine upon the green plants of the brookside lest the natural man grow too strong.

A KINSMAN (Father's Side)

Here is Meriasek worshipping Almighty God at the very summit of the mountain. As the old people reckon it, this chapel stands at an elevation of half a mile or more.

COUNT OF ROHAN

Joy to you, Meriasek. The purpose of our visit is not only to brighten your day but also to offer encouragement and to let you know that as your kinsmen we are concerned for you.

MERIASEK

Why are you concerned? To my knowledge, I have not intentionally harmed you or anyone else, nor would I ever want to, the Blessed Lord helping me.

COUNT OF ROHAN

It seems to us a great pity that you, a man of such lofty descent, should choose to live here under circumstances so mean and comfortless. I say you are no friend to yourself.

MERIASEK

For me the greatest good is to draw near to God; to worship Him, to do His will as it ought to be done and thereby hope to inherit the Kingdom of Heaven.

KINSMAN (Mother's Side)

You could worship God and yet live pleasantly and decently as many are doing these days. Do leave this place and come away with us. Alas, it is pitiful to see you merely existing here, like an animal.

MERIASEK

Poverty for the Lord's sake here on earth makes for advancement at the court of the hereafter. It is likewise the mother of well-being. You fail to comprehend, my children, how the soul is nourished to the full.

COUNT OF ROHAN

You are being foolish, Meriasek. Surely you could worship God while occupying a position of honor in the world. All who are dear to you are ashamed to think of you stuck away here in beggarly contentment.

MERIASEK

Slow down a bit, good people! This humbled existence leads toward an exalted life in aftertime, and through it the soul is nourished unto perfect salvation.

It subdues the lusts of the flesh and enables the world to be trodden under foot. It harms no living thing and ever confounds the devil's power. Beyond all doubt, it feeds the soul and opens the way to heaven's joy.

COUNT OF ROHAN

Yet there are surely a large number of people who entertain hope of heaven while also valuing the things of this world. Like them, you could bring great credit to your family without sacrificing the salvation of your soul.

MERIASEK

By my faith, I have never cared for earthly possessions, influence, or wealth. They are a delusion and a snare. To you who have them in abundance, I say, beware! They are not to be trusted.

KINSMAN (Father's Side)

Do not press the man any further. The dear Christ must be faithfully served. If Meriasek were not a true saint, it is plain that he could not have performed so many miracles.

COUNT OF ROHAN

I shan't persist since, obviously, it's useless to do so. However, on the strength of the blood-tie between us, Meriasek, I earnestly entreat you to do one thing for me. The country is infested with robbers, who have already committed numerous murders. Rid us of them through your extraordinary powers.

At present, no one can attend a fair without being robbed, robbed, indeed, of both his goods and his life. But if you are willing to help me, I should like to have several annual fairs here in Brittany.

The first of them would take place on the sixth day of July; the second on the eighth of August;[54] and I want the third to be at Michaelmas in September. All three are to be permanently assigned to the parish of Noyal.[55]

MERIASEK

Through God's grace alone, your wish shall be granted exactly as you have expressed it. The robbers shall be forced to go elsewhere, those who ask God's mercy turning to better ways.
(Count of Rohan goes away home and Meriasek waits in the same place.)

FIRST OUTLAW

Now, men, have a look around. Bless me, if you see anybody on the move in these woods, hustle his purse to me. God curse the man who talks against plundering.[56]
(Here fire comes upon them.)

SECOND OUTLAW

Oh! Oh! Woe to us, one and all, the whole forest is afire. We'll be burnt to ashes! This comes to pay us back for the devil's work we've done.

THIRD OUTLAW

Hey, shut up, the devil roast you! What's all the flap about? I know, if you don't, that the only glare is the rising moon!

FOURTH OUTLAW

Out of here! Out of here! Let's run for it. The woods are blazing up into one huge bonfire!
(Horse ready)
Out! Out, or we'll be roasted! I'm getting away as quick as I can. God damn it all, where's that black horse of mine? May the devil nag him!
(Let the fourth outlaw go off on the horse.)

FIRST OUTLAW

O Meriasek, Meriasek, mighty saint, only pray that I be saved from the fire and I will serve you for life!

SECOND OUTLAW

Save me, Meriasek, oh, save me! If what they say is true, your power is great. I will serve you from now on if I am spared.

THIRD OUTLAW

Meriasek, as a true saint, save my life, and it shall be yours.

FIFTH OUTLAW

I have faith in Meriasek and his power. I will be his servant, and for my stinking sins will beg, "Have mercy on me, Jesus."

FIRST OUTLAW

Thanks to Christ and Meriasek, we are completely saved from harm this time. We will go to him and ask him outright to beg Christ to forgive us....

(To Meriasek on the mountain)
Joy to you, Meriasek. We have come to ask your advice. As depraved men, we have led revoltingly wicked lives, robbing and plundering many.

But when we went into the forest today, intending as usual to rob entirely innocent people, a stroke of fiery lightning came down on us. It seemed we were like to be burnt up on the instant.

I cried piteously, "Help me, Meriasek!" That saved me and some of my mates along with me. Others ran away, I don't know where. So here I am, struck all of a heap. What, alas, if I be lost forever!

MERIASEK

Ask Jesus for mercy, never forgetting your God; be at pains to make a full confession; turn to sin no more, and very willingly will I pray for you to Christ Jesus.

FIRST OUTLAW

Oh, Meriasek, if it is possible, take pity on us poor souls. Had we not called upon your name, all of us, young and old, would have been lost.
(He ends.)

MERIASEK

Never despair. God is merciful to as many as will call upon His Name. Since you are penitent, I will bless you *in nomine patris et filii et spiritus sancti amen.* Seize every opportunity to make restitution to those you have wronged.

COUNT OF ROHAN

Thanks be to Jesus and likewise to Meriasek, peace has been restored to us all. Rich as well as poor can now visit the fairs; the robbers, it is certain, have left the country far behind them.

For this we owe thanks to the might of Jesus invoked through the prayers of Meriasek. The three fairs are to be held in this country annually from now on; Meriasek has granted them. May his name be venerated for all time to come. As I had wished, the first fair shall be held on the sixth of July, the second on the eighth of August, while the third is appointed for September twenty-ninth, St. Michael's Feast Day, and shall take place in the blissful parish of Noyal. At each of these fairs, the name of Meriasek shall be kept in remembrance forever.

(Here the Duke of Cornwall shall parade, saying:)

DUKE OF CORNWALL

I am the Duke of Cornwall, as was my father before me, lord supreme over this domain from Tamar to Land's End.[57] For the present, I am at Castle an Dynas, Pydar Hundred,[58] and on high ground up country I have another castle which is called Tintagel.[59] That is my principal residence.

It has reached my ears that in Penwith Hundred[60] there is a man of great saintliness who has recently arrived from across the water. Tell me, Steward, have you had reliable news of him?

THE DUKE'S STEWARD

I have, mighty lord. His name is Meriasek, a man of thorough-going sanctity. According to the report, he is beloved by all who know him and has done a great deal of good in the area.

THE DUKE'S CHAMBERLAIN

My lord, the fact is that the man has left us for foreign parts. Since a week ago, no one has seen him in Cornwall.

DUKE

Why should he leave the country, a man who has always led a most exemplary life? One has never heard anything to the contrary. He seems never to have uttered a base word and as for his deeds, many have praised his outstanding kindness.

THE DUKE'S CHAMBERLAIN

As you are aware, a wicked pagan named Teudar has recently landed on our shores.[61] A man of shocking cruelty, he will not allow a Christian within his bailiwick. He has doubtless driven Meriasek away.

DUKE

Fie, a thousand times fie on the filthy hound! Why wasn't I informed of this sooner? By the Lord who gave me the breath of life, I'll cut his breath exceedingly short! Before Wednesday nightfall

69

he shall come to grief, winning nothing, losing everything, so that his teeth will chatter.

Let my household be ready. I won't tolerate the dog's presence in my shire. He shall pay dearly for his intrusion, and if he refuses to withdraw, his blood will pour down to the ground.

THE DUKE'S STEWARD

We are in readiness, your grace. He has already done much harm since he came here. His home base is in Meneage, no doubt at Lesteader,[62] where many are rallying to him.

DUKE

Even if he should have a hundred thousand, they shall die to the last man in the name of Christ on high. I will know the reason for his coming into this country without my express permission. Courage, my men, and forward to our goal!
(The duke descends with twenty armed men bearing streamers.)
In what direction would it be best to proceed, my lords, in order to confront the tyrant? If I can manage it, he shall fare badly because he is certain to find himself powerless against Christians.

STEWARD

He *was* living at Lesteader in Meneage, but the rascal has another place called Goodern.[63] That's in Powder. For the time being, the nasty fellow is holed up there.

DUKE

In the name of Christ on high, we will continue southward. If he is still in Cornwall, we shall assuredly meet up with the villain. Unfurl my banner before me. As becomes a worthy leader, I will advance.

(To Teudar)

SECOND MESSENGER

Hail, Teudar, noble emperor! There is a duke of this territory who has risen against you and with him a great host. He boasts that he will surely see you dead.

70

EMPEROR TEUDAR

Down with the filthy pretender! I defy him through every hour of the day and night. They shall tremble behind their beards. To arms, executioners! Forward! Woe to the caitiff!

FIRST EXECUTIONER

(He goes down to Teudar.)

We are armed and ready. They'll indeed shake in their beards who raise a hand against you. If we need to hold our ground, I say the devil himself hasn't the nerve to spar with us!

TEUDAR

Let us take the field, in the devil's name, with no crossing of ourselves at any time. By my soul, they're going to pay for it, the duke and those men of his, before we knock off work, *par mon ame*! I have fifteen thousand men at my disposal. In truth, more than fifteen thousand.

(He descends with fifteen armed men bearing streamers.)

(Here a demon shall parade.)

FIRST DEMON

Silence, I say, silence both far and near! Give ear to Jupiter, your Holy Father of the North.[64] A multitude of those who serve me are approaching. Beelzebub, we will go to set their feet on the right path.

SECOND DEMON, BEELZEBUB

Master, that's a sound course of action. With our encouragement, Teudar will do quite a satisfactory amount of harm. Shall we go to meet him at the temple? One thing is sure, I'm at my best when doing my worst.

(Let him go into the temple.)

TEUDAR

(They all kneel.)

Joy to you, divine Monfras![65] I seek your blessing on the eve of battle. May I never be a good-doer nor ever give the idea a thought.

FIRST DEMON

My dear Teudar, conduct yourself like a true man, never deserting the wrong. I will help you, and your soul shall be secure. I have prepared a hole for it and for the souls of all your fighting men. Rejoice! The more you kill now, the greater your prestige later.

FIRST EXECUTIONER

Let's be on our way at once. No matter how we behave, we'll always belong to Mohammed.

STEWARD

My lord duke, I see Teudar and his mob of cutthroats. Do you wish to question him as to his business in this country?

DUKE OF CORNWALL

I do, steward, truly. Though he prove a magician, I shan't ever fear him; though they are offering a show of force, I shall gentle them and subdue them.
(To the enemy vanguard)
Pagan tyrant, by what right are you in this country? It is obvious you can advance neither title nor claim through inheritance from either parent. And further, you have driven out that ever-saintly man, Meriasek.

TEUDAR

Before I'm done, I shall drive you out of the country just as I did Meriasek if it turns out that you're another worshipper of that dirty-mouthed pretender called Jesus, who experienced grim agonies on a cross. I'm for taking vengeance on his followers as a matter of course. I have come, frozen-face, to do away with every last one of them.

DUKE

That, you false, unbelieving dog, you are not strong enough to do. To the contrary, it is I who will shed your blood. My life on it, I'll have you chopped as fine as greens in a soup. I understand that in your own country you were a nursemaid to horses. What, does a

72

devil's spawn like you think of avenging himself on the Duke of Cornwall?

TEUDAR

The Duke of Cornwall and all his men I will mash underfoot like so much pulp! However modest my property may have been at home, I have certainly added to it here. I am a conqueror, an able warrior, furthermore, who is feared among those of high degree.

DUKE

To me, your power isn't worth a single, sterile bean, you bully! If you don't remove yourself from my territory at once, I shall run you through the heart. I'm convinced you were riff-raff at home, an out-and-out rascal. Beg for pardon, dog, or get out of my sight!

How does a foreigner like you dare to attack Christians? I'll beat the dandruff off your scaly noggin in clouds and hear you rue the day you ever crossed my path.

TEUDAR

Faith, a midge would swallow a horse if only it could, the same as a sot like you looks to damage a man like me if only I'd stand still for it. But I won't, you bastard, since I can call on nothing less than kings for help.

DUKE

You'll get precious little help from your blasted kings. Go ahead, send for the lot and for all your petty knights and lords. As Christ's faithful servants, I and all my people will await you on the field of battle.

TEUDAR

Let's have no rubbishy prattle about Christ in my hearing, you loathsome idiot, or you and your gang will smart for it, you rotten specimen of knighthood! Do you imagine, eh, that you can stand up against an emperor?

DUKE

Aagh! There's no knowing whether a tricky renegade of your sort

73

was born with so much as a nook of land to your name. So don't imagine, alien scum, that you can lord it by day or by night within the borders of my inheritance. For meddling with such a saintly man as blessed Meriasek, you are going to fare very badly indeed. By the Aweful Day of Judgment, I say that to me, horse-boy, you're a total good-for-nothing!

TEUDAR

You will either deny your faith, Duke, or find yourself my prisoner before dark. King Alwar, King Pygys, His Illustrious Majesty King Mark, and a sovereign whose name is Casvelyn are approaching to join forces with me.[66]

DUKE

Let them come whenever they like, they will matter very little here since not a one will get away alive. Through the grace of Almighty God, we shall be a match for you were you a hundred thousand strong. We want nothing better than a chance to do battle against the enemies of Christ in the name of Christ!

TEUDAR

I defy Christ, I defy you and every Christian in your train! You're a pack of rascals! Soldiers, in return for their daring to oppose me, break these Christians' heads for them straightway!

DUKE

Come on, then, as soon as you please. In the name of Christ and his mercy, I am ready to give as good as I get. Fall upon them, men! They shall have good reason to remember us before they die.... (*Guns.*[67] *Here they shall fight and a horse ready.*)

TEUDAR

A horse, men, fetch me a horse! It's impossible to resist longer, my people killed and I with an ugly wound. I despised the duke, but he's a good fighter, the strongest and steadiest I've ever encountered.

DUKE

Ho, soldiers, cease the attack! The tyrant has broken and run away. He couldn't withstand me or his losses. Glory to Christ who gave us the victory!
(He goes up.)

Peace to all of you here present. Today you have witnessed a portion of Meriasek's life. Return in good time tomorrow when, by God's grace, the remainder of a saintly life will be revealed.

We heartily urge you to refresh yourselves for the benefit of the play and may you have, good men and women, the blessing of Christ and Meriasek, likewise of Mary of Camborne. Musicians, now play with a will that we may dance.

PROLOGUE TO DAY TWO[68]

(On the second day the Emperor Constantine[69] shall here parade, saying:)

CONSTANTINE

I am Constantine. Here in Rome, the world's greatest city, I assumed the emperor's crown and was converted to Christianity by Silvester. Throughout my dominions, I decree that the worship of unprofitable gods be abandoned in favor of Christ who, in the fullness of his grace, redeemed us on the Cross.

(Here the blind Count Globus[70] begins, saying:)

COUNT

How great, O God, is my affliction! Of what value is all my wealth when I am blind? Lead me, therefore, to Meriasek. I have heard that he is a mighty doer of miracles. If he will consent to cure me, he shall have a handsome reward.

SQUIRE OF COUNT GLOBUS

I will take you to him. If Jesus wills, our errand shall succeed. Let us go to the mountain without delay and, my lord, be open with Meriasek about your handicap.
(A staff in his hand, let the count go over to Meriasek's mountain, his squire leading him.)

COUNT

May God in heaven come to my aid and give me sight....

MERIASEK

May the Lord, maker of land and sea, ever sustain me and guide my feet in the paths of righteousness. Lord Jesus, look down from heaven and grant me never-failing grace. Jesus, to serve you is the whole desire of my life on earth.

COUNT

Joy to you, Meriasek. You are very rightly regarded as a man of virtuous life, and your fellow-countrymen are unanimous in accounting you a kind and generous priest toward rich and poor alike, ever ready to help those in need.

I am blind. Although I venture to speak to you, I cannot see you. I entreat you to banish my darkness, and if it is within my power, I desire to reward you for it. Lacking the use of my eyes, I am dependent upon others. If, now, you see fit to give me your aid, you shall never want for things of this world.

MERIASEK

I take no interest in worldly goods nor am I inclined to help either the rich or the poor because of the return involved. Earthly possessions are an illusion, pure and simple. To care about them is to care about precious little.

COUNT

I am very much surprised to learn that you have no regard for this world's goods. No man, including yourself, can live for long without them. They are a passport to acceptance by the nobility and a means of retaining their respect.

Ask me for as much as you please, Meriasek. You shan't be stinted though you were to demand a hundred pounds. If you will fully restore my sight, I will pay you in gold.

MERIASEK

No man on earth may sell God's grace, my son. If one gives thought to the matter, a better way reveals itself.

COUNT

I am not concerned about the money I have offered you. If only I had the use of my eyes, I wouldn't be afraid to hold up my end in a haggle with a king. Not in the least. The truth is I'd rather be able to see than have an income property worth ten pounds a year,[71] yes, even if I were to give it to you in perpetuity.

MERIASEK

Continue to keep all that you have offered, whether gold or land. As for me, while life lasts I shall follow in the footsteps of Christ, holiest of the holy.

COUNT

I most earnestly entreat you to heal me for the sake of the Passion which Jesus underwent on earth: scourged by the Jews, nailed through hands and feet, with a sharp lance pierced to the heart so that the blood poured down. Make a blind man truly whole for love of Jesus Christ.

MERIASEK

I look on all your riches as worth less than a handful of beans. But had you appealed to me earlier through the love I bear toward Jesus, you would already have been healed.
(He kneels.)

Christ Jesus, Christ Jesus, full of mercy, give this man his sight, I implore.

COUNT

(He kneels.)

May Christ, the Lord Almighty, be worshipped forever, and

glorious Saint Meriasek, in his beauty and honor. They have made me whole. I now see everything full and clear. Never was my sight better. As all of us know, whether cleric or layman, in this man God has a faithful servant.

A DEMONIAC

(A devil ready by his side.)

For the love of Christ, oh, help me, Meriasek! I am mercilessly plagued by an evil spirit. My life is not worth living. It seizes me in sudden fits, so that were I to be burnt alive, it would be less of an ordeal than these fits.

A DEAF MAN

I am a man who is deaf while you, Meriasek, are a man who is sanctified, which leads me to think that you could, if you wished, cure my deafness here and now. For the love of Christ, the Son of Grace, pay heed to us, the unfortunate.
(He kneels.)

MERIASEK

Christ Jesus, should there be an evil spirit lurking near, in mercy banish it to its appointed place and grant healing to these men here present as a witness that I am your servant on earth.

DEVIL

(He howls.)[72]

Away with you, Meriasek, out of my sight! Curses on you for the mischief you have done me everywhere hereabouts. I never have a moment's peace on account of you. Yet in spite of you and your lying mouth, I'll go right on spreading disease!

DEMONIAC

Thanks be to Jesus! The evil spirit has gone out of me. I am well again, free from all distress! Meriasek, for as long as I live, I'm indebted to you.

DEAF MAN

And I can really hear now! I'm your debtor for life, Meriasek. You have completely restored us to health.

COUNT

May your name be praised, Meriasek. You have lifted from us our heavy burden of distress and brought us great joy. We pray that Christ will always nourish and protect your power for good.

MERIASEK

Go home now, dear children. My blessing goes with you always. Don't make me late for my devotions and never forget to give thanks to God. Ever bear in mind that it is God who has cured you, not I.
(All proceed home.)

(Here the Count of Vannes shall parade.)

COUNT

I am the Count of Vannes, a title of much dignity. Glory to God in the highest and may I be granted the grace to uphold that glory. Because the bishop of this area[73] has lately died, I shall pay a visit to the college. My immediate consideration must be given to the choice of our next bishop.

SQUIRE OF THE COUNT OF VANNES

Surely very little gets done in this country, my lord, without you. We will accompany you. It would appear that all ranks are in favor of Meriasek for bishop.
(The count goes down.)

COUNT OF VANNES

(To the Dean in the chapter house on the platea.)
Greetings, reverend sir, and to your chapter. I have come, agreeable to your advice, to learn who shall be chosen as our bishop.

DEAN

My honored lord, you are sincerely welcome here. We shall be gratified to have your opinion as to the best choice of a bishop to lead us.

COUNT OF VANNES

The voice of the people calls loudly for the elevation of Meriasek, and for my part I know of no better man for the vacancy. If there are those present who think otherwise, let us hear from them now.

A CANON

We would be most happy to obtain Meriasek as our overseer, a man of his saintliness being anything but a disappointment to us. Send for his bulls, my dear lord.

COUNT OF VANNES

Come forward, messenger. Go in my name to Pope Silvester and say that the leading men of Brittany are petitioning His Holiness in behalf of Meriasek, an outstanding man. We should be gratified to have him as bishop of Vannes, with as little delay as possible.

MESSENGER

(To the Count of Vannes)
My lord count, your hopes will not be disappointed. I shall return with the bulls, traveling rapidly and lingering nowhere. Farewell to you.
(The Count goes home.)[74]

SILVESTER

May the power of God the Father ever sustain us. May Jesus Christ, the Son, in the fullness of his grace, come to our aid by day and by night. That we may have the comfort of the blessed Holy Spirit always with us, Mary, Mother and Virgin, invoke God's mercy upon us.

His mercy is ever available to man if man will seek it. It is not according to God's will that those he has redeemed should be lost.

Up, therefore, be cleansed by full confession, avoid sin in this world, fully repent the sin you fail to avoid, and take care never to repeat it. In so doing you shall surely come to that joy without equal which is in heaven.

MESSENGER[75]

Silvester, my most respectful greetings. I have been sent here from Brittany to seek your authority, my good lord, for the consecration of Meriasek as bishop of the fair city of Vannes. It is the wish of the nobles.

SILVESTER

You are welcome, my dear son. Meriasek is known to us by reputation as a man of saintly qualities. His bulls shall be prepared for you at once so that you may begin your return journey as soon as possible....
(Bulls ready.)

A CARDINAL

(To the messenger)
The bulls are inscribed. Messenger, take custody of them by license of my dear lord, Silvester. Concerning Meriasek there is indeed much of good report.

MESSENGER

Many thanks to you, my lord Silvester, for your graciousness in expediting my errand. I now beg leave to return home.

SILVESTER

Christ's blessing go with you. Convey my greetings to the lords of Brittany and to Meriasek. In very truth he is a saintly man. No one now living, man or woman, could have a better shepherd than he.

MESSENGER

(To the Count of Vannes)
Hail, my lord count, in your tower! I have discharged my mission

to the letter. Receive the bulls into your safe-keeping. When I spoke of Meriasek, the Pope lauded him.

COUNT OF VANNES

Welcome, messenger. Now let a delegation proceed to the wilderness and bring Meriasek to us. Convey to him a letter saying that our nobles are resolved to elevate him to high rank.

DEAN

It shall be done, my lord. Let us be on our way to Meriasek as speedily as possible. Still in the wild though he is, he shall emerge from his wretchedness if he chooses....
(At the mountain to Meriasek)
Joy to you, Meriasek. Here is a fair-written letter for you, something to be read at once. To a man, the nobles want you to become bishop of Vannes.

MERIASEK

My profound thanks to all the lords, and to you, most worshipful canons. I do not, however, aspire to that particular honor nor ever to hold a benefice or other charge of any kind as long as I live.

A CANON

You are not being realistic, Meriasek. Once you are a right reverend bishop, your life becomes princely. You will enjoy a spendable income of three hundred pounds a year and more. Your bulls are already in hand, and you won't be out of pocket at all.

MERIASEK

Your attitude closely resembles that of many others in Holy Church today. When they seek preferment, the first consideration is how much money can be had from it. They forget that strict account which must be rendered when each of us comes before Christ at the Judgment.

Let him who holds a cure of souls give heed and remember this: one day an accounting will surely be required of him, and if a defect be charged to a pastor and proved against him, woe to him against whom the charge is proved!

The more searching the record, the longer, as you all know, the reading of it is certain to be. For myself, I wish no cure save of one soul. God grant that I may faithfully rule that one!

DEAN

My brethren, let us go home. This man will not listen to those who wish him well....
(To the Count of Vannes)
My lord count, Meriasek refuses to become our father in God or even take charge of a congregation.
(He goes up and waits in place.)

COUNT OF VANNES

Alas, how are we to deal with him? We are greatly astonished to learn that he declines the dignity. We must find a way to bring him round, or I shall be displeased.

(Here the Bishop of Cornouaille shall parade if he wishes.)

BISHOP OF CORNOUAILLE

I am Brittany's Bishop of Cornouaille, a worthy prelate. It is my wish to journey to Vannes and join the lords assembled there.

THE BISHOP'S CROZIER-BEARER

There is much to be done at Vannes, certainly. It is needful to obtain the advice of dedicated men like yourself as to who shall be consecrated bishop. Meanwhile, the fact of Meriasek's nomination is known.
(He goes down. Here the Second Bishop shall parade.)

SECOND BISHOP

Crozier-bearer, let us proceed to Vannes. There is much discussion about a new bishop for the district. The choice has fallen to Meriasek but, as I hear it, he will not accept.

SECOND CROZIER-BEARER

By St. John, my lord, if anyone gave me such a chance, I would seize it gladly, and I'd put nobles in the traces.[76] There would be no

call to urge me further.
(The Second Bishop comes down. Count Globus descends.)

COUNT GLOBUS

Bon jour, my lord bishop of Cornouaille. I earnestly entreat you and your company to go with us to Vannes.

BISHOP OF CORNOUAILLE

Welcome, count, by this same good day. Welcome, esteemed bishop, and welcome to all who are with you.

SECOND BISHOP

Thank you both very much indeed, noble sirs. It appears we are all headed in the one direction, which is to Vannes, where there is a good deal awaiting our attention, unless my ears have deceived me.

COUNT GLOBUS

(To the Count of Vannes)
Joy to you, count, and my respects to the entire chapter, whatever their degree. We have journeyed here from home with the desire of elevating Meriasek.

COUNT OF VANNES

Welcome, kind and noble sir, and welcome to you, my lords bishop. We are much perplexed. Meriasek has, indeed, been chosen for consecration as bishop, but he has summarily declined the honor.
(All go down with the Count of Vannes.)

BISHOP OF CORNOUAILLE

If his bulls have been received, he shall be consecrated bishop. God forbid that it should be otherwise! Why will he not accept? As bishop he can help and benefit all the people in his charge.

SECOND BISHOP

Let it be put to him a second time in case he can thus be persuaded to accept the dignity. We know for a fact that he is unanimously regarded by his countrymen as a man of exemplary life.

COUNT GLOBUS

Then we will go to him without further discussion, and make sure that we bring him back with us. Among the worthy and the blessed he stands high.

BISHOP OF CORNOUAILLE

Since on that score we are all agreed, let us go together in a body, whatever our rank and station. Every one, be he layman or cleric, shall witness the attempt we make....
(Let him go across to the hermitage on the mountain.) [77]

SECOND BISHOP

Here is Meriasek. My lord count, you should speak to him first with the voice of your great authority. If through mildness we can persuade him to come with us of his own free will, it would be a pity to distress him.

COUNT OF VANNES

(To Meriasek)
Joy to you, Meriasek. For a long time you have lived here in utter poverty. But now through your humility you are raised to greatness as a saint among men.

COUNT GLOBUS

Among your countrymen you are seen as a man of exemplary life and noble lineage. Surely it is not right for you to remain here in such miserable circumstances. Therefore, come away with us.

SECOND BISHOP

The papal bulls have been received. We have authority to consecrate you Bishop of Vannes in conformity with the will of the populace. It constitutes, indeed, a lifelong bond between you and them.

MERIASEK

For the love of Christ on high, do not speak to me of preferment. I do not wish ever to become a bishop nor ever undertake the cure of any human soul except my own. Lords, lords, go home! No longer hinder my devotions.

BISHOP OF CORNOUAILLE

In view of the fact that your consecration has already been ordained by the Pope, do not try to argue or set yourself against us. Willing or not, you shall say goodbye to this place and depart with us.

MERIASEK

(He is being led.)
Blessed Mary, help me! Mary, they are leading me away from you against my will. Mary, Mother and Virgin, you know how the very thought of this burden saddens me!

COUNT OF VANNES

You are being foolish, Meriasek. The cure of souls in this region must be undertaken by somebody, for where the shepherd is lax, the fox is certain to prey upon the sheep.

Since we are of one mind, let us invest him with due honor and authority in Saint Samson's church.[78] This is the only right thing to do, Meriasek, so do not agitate yourself further....

MERIASEK

(In the Dean's church)
For the sake of the Passion which Jesus suffered for us, hands and feet nailed to a cross by the Jews, the blood in the veins flowing from the spearthrust to the heart, the skull pierced through by a crown of thorns — for the sake of Him who bore these things, I now beg of you that I may never become a bishop. God has granted me no knowledge of His will concerning such an obligation.

BISHOP OF CORNOUAILLE

No longer bandy futile words with us. Approach, seat yourself upon your throne, and assume the robes of office. We shall clothe you as befits a worthy prelate. You will lack nothing that is needful.

(Here Meriasek wears a gown.)

SECOND BISHOP

Take the pastoral staff into your hand in the name of Christ on high and Mary ever virgin.

(A pastoral staff of silver and a mitre ready.)

Let us place the mitre on his head, happy witnesses to his investiture.

BISHOP OF CORNOUAILLE

And now the blessing. May Jesus Christ, Son of Mary, ever guide you in accordance with His will. As of this moment, you are become the shepherd of your people. Noble folk, with this installation a bright day has dawned.

COUNT OF VANNES

Now are we all gratified that Meriasek is ordained as our bishop, a prince of the church among us, defender of the faith, a source of help to multitudes.

MERIASEK THE BISHOP

The dignity thus bestowed upon me seems, in my eyes, more a shame than an honor. As God is my witness, I am not well pleased to have it. I have no taste for the rewards of this world....

A NAKED SICK MAN

God save you, worthy people! For the sake of the Passion which Christ, the Virgin's Son endured: a spear thrust to the heart, nailed hand and foot to a cross between a pair of thieves, crowned with thorns whose spines pierced through to the brain; for love of Him, give me a garment with which to cover myself. I am naked and the wind is cold.

COUNT OF VANNES

Have the goodness to raise your clamor somewhere else, my man. It is most unseemly to come into the presence of the lords naked as you are and with your body a mass of sores from head to foot. Rarely, if ever, have I seen a person whose limbs were more diseased than yours.

NAKED MAN

Oh, by the numberless wounds that Christ endured for man's salvation, give heed to my hapless, rotted flesh, my ruptured veins! Scarcely a living soul befriends me.

Many's the snowy and icy night I've spent in the open when even the ground was frozen, while my sores, brimming with foulness, burned and burned. Because I am so eaten up with corruption, no one will give me a place to lay my head.

BISHOP MERIASEK

Though I were to go naked, you shall be clothed. How pitiful the sight of your flesh gone bad like sheep-rot.

NAKED MAN

Truly, so great is my plight, and I have become so feeble, the only thing I wish for is a decent death. But Death will not look at me. He shuns me because I am diseased.

BISHOP MERIASEK

Now, good man, may Jesus grant you health from head to foot, and for the strengthening of the Faith, Jesus, Lord of Salvation, heal this man by divine remedy. Cover your nakedness with this garment and be comforted.

(A gown or mantle upon the Naked Man.)

NAKED MAN

The mighty Lord Jesus reward you, Meriasek! I am healed. Not one sore is left anywhere on my body, and all my rotting flesh has been restored to health and that painlessly!

COUNT OF VANNES

Honor to you, Meriasek! We did not realize the true greatness of your power here on earth. Your new dignity becomes you. As for us, we will go our separate ways.

(Let the count and his retinue go off homeward.)

BISHOP MERIASEK

God's blessing go with you. Touching the dignity you have bestowed upon me here, I would gladly give it to another man, as God is my witness.
(Then let all go away home.)

FIRST LEPER

Lord of heaven, what am I to do? I am so leprous that everyone shrinks from the sight of me. Still, they say that Meriasek is willing and able to cure poor people whatever their disease. I will pluck up my courage and go and seek his help.

SECOND LEPER

(To Meriasek)

God bless you, Meriasek! As you do not need to be told, we two are segregated lepers. For the love of Christ on high, we beg you to heal us.

MERIASEK'S CHAPLAIN

Stay where you are! It is not seemly for lepers to draw near to persons of quality. It behooves you to keep your distance and await the alms of His Worship.

BISHOP MERIASEK

Oh, my dear chaplain, let us have no further reproof of the poor and unfortunate who come to me. I am more disposed to welcome them than the greatest lords of the realm, believe me.

What do you wish to say, lepers? If you have business with me, speak out in the name of the Most High.

FIRST LEPER

For the love of the King of Heaven, help us to conquer our disease. We are segregated lepers. According to report, you are a holy man, ever willing to help God's people.

BISHOP MERIASEK

(He kneels.)

Mary, Queen of Heaven, intercede for me with Christ, the gracious. Mary, aid these needy ones against their affliction. Mary, even as I humbly call upon you, heal these two persons in both face and body. May the Mother of God, whom I serve, restore you to health.

FIRST LEPER

Thanks be to Jesus! You are healed, my comrade, all your skin come clean and fair.

SECOND LEPER

And so it is with you as well! Never have I seen anyone more free of blemish, more spotless, thanks to Jesus. To you, Meriasek, a man blessed by his works, deepest respect.

BISHOP MERIASEK

Make your way homeward now, my children, and give thanks not to me but to Christ alone. Pin your faith to this: Jesus ever helps us all, whether we be weak or strong.
(*Let him exit.*)

INTERLUDE OF MARY AND THE WOMAN'S SON[79]

(*Here King Massen shall parade.*)

KING MASSEN

I am King Massen,[80] in all my days and ways a stout-hearted lord. Every Thursday I like to go hunting in the forest. So, Huntsman, get your hounds ready, and men of my household, layman and cleric alike, prepare yourselves to accompany me.

THE KING'S FIRST HUNTSMAN

My lord, we'll be ready. Gaze-hounds or trace-hounds, I have plenty of both. If we were to bring a stag to bay, you can believe it would be dispatched at once.
(*He ends.*)

(Here a certain woman's son, as is found in The Miracles of the Blessed Mary,[81] *shall parade, saying:)*

THE WOMAN'S SON

A young man owes it to himself to mingle with the nobility. In their society he can improve himself, learning what is manly and profitable. I'm eager to set out for the king's court without delay. Farewell, dear mother.

THE WOMAN

My son, may the blessing of Mary be with you. As I hope to live, I'd rather have you stay here at home with me. But as it is, I'll go and implore Mary, the Mother of Mercies, to watch over both you and me.
(Let her go over to the church.)
Mary, joy to you and glory forevermore. Beloved Mary, succor and sustain me in this my earthly life. Mary, I have only the one child, a son, to hold me dear. Keep him in your care, for all my trust is in you....

SON

(To King Massen)
Hail, my lord king! Of my own free will I have come to offer service as is my duty. If at any time you are pleased to call upon me, I will discharge the trust whatever the pay.

KING

Welcome, loyal henchman. We are about to go hunting in open country, where there is known to be an evil tyrant. Although I should prefer not to encounter him, let every man take along his weapons.
(He goes down with the armed men.)

(Here the tyrant shall parade, saying:)

TYRANT

I rule alone, a prince without equal under the sun. No matter how formidable he might be, no mortal man could stand against

91

me. It now pleases me to amuse myself with hunting in the forest. All get ready, high and low alike, to go with me.

FIRST KNIGHT OF THE TYRANT

My most powerful lord, we are prepared to follow you into the forest. Your hounds are on leash and every man properly equipped, hundreds of us in arms.

SECOND KNIGHT OF THE TYRANT

Even the little hounds on hand would put away five chopped-up steers within two days. There's Swallow-His-Spoon and Lick-Tub, Skirly-Whirly (he's a tawny hound), Blackbeard, and shapely Brindle.
(Let him go down.)

KING MASSEN

Now, huntsmen, keep your eyes moving. If you sight game, release your hounds at once, and good luck to you!

KING'S FIRST HUNTSMAN[82]

I see a large body of men. Something tells me they're up to no good.
(The hart ready in the wood.)

KING

Hold! I see a hart, which will very soon be down, never fear.

KING'S SECOND HUNTSMAN

Majesty, do not forget caution. It is the tyrant, surely, and he has risen against you.

KING

Then we shall respond. Let us take up our position here, my soldiers, every man at the ready.
(And the hart hunted.)

(Here the executioners shall parade.)

FIRST EXECUTIONER

Let's not be slack, comrades, the word being that the tyrant has, for a fact, gone off to the forest. We'd better follow along, else we're sure to be blamed and draw punishment besides.

SECOND EXECUTIONER

If he sent us an order, it's our job to show up, that's for sure. But personally, I wouldn't know whether he's gone from home or not. Maybe that boy of ours, the filthy little bastard, could find out.

THIRD EXECUTIONER

Let's send the boy, a speedy one amongst the litter, to see if the head man's from home, and he can come back and tell us. All the same, the man pays rotten wages, by my soul!

FIRST EXECUTIONER

So we've got a right to drag our feet. We can't pay up better because we aren't paid better. If he won't improve as master, then we'll not stay long in his service, my life on it!

SECOND EXECUTIONER

Hey, boy, you rascal you, go find out whether the head man wants to visit the forest, and come back and tell us so's we can join in and give him some help.

THIRD EXECUTIONER

Mind you don't dawdle on the way, boy. Meantime, let's go and wet our whistles, good lads, while Toby's[83] gone, God blast his carcass! Out of a thousand no-goods, he's the worst.
(Let the three executioners go over to the tent near that of the Woman's Son.)

THE MENIAL

Well, you're not going to be any too merry after this errand's done....

My lord tyrant, sir, for lack of wages your 'pages' refuse to stir one step from home.

TYRANT

What! Has it come to that? If I have to go and fetch them, I'll pay them off in blows. They'll step lively then though every muscle in their bodies pains them. Look sharp and find us each a switch.

MENIAL

'pon my life, most excellent lord, that's a splendid idea! Here are the switches and may there be no holding back. Let them be paid in full for their impudence.

TYRANT

(At the executioners' tent)

Ho, sirs, who's at home? Here's a nest without an egg. Devil take the retainer who hides. Where could they have gone? By Moham-med, the mighty, my trouble grows double!

MENIAL

I'll lead you right to them, to the tavern where they're dead sure to be drinking, red to the gills.

Lord, let me make a suggestion. Whale them, each of them, till their arses ache.

(He shouts into another tent.)

Ho, masters, is there a drop left? I've got news for you. Your errand is all taken care of. Faith, there's wages coming to you, the kind you can really feel. So now if there's a sip left for me, pass it here.

FIRST EXECUTIONER

Ah, welcome back, sot! What does the stinker say? Must I run to him? Come in and sample the pot. It'll cost you a groat[84] before leaving, so help me!

SECOND EXECUTIONER

We've drunk too much, by God, and there's too few to pay the bill. God damn the master, he's so slow with the wages, we're left all the farther behind! And you can't reason with him, neither.

THIRD EXECUTIONER

Hey, boy, how come you didn't bring our money back with you? No wages, no can get along. Nine nobles[85] from May Day would have done us some good.

TYRANT

Well, well, I will pay your score or else forfeit my hat. By my soul, not too many are going to laugh! Now, Toby, help me. Until we hear them say they're sorry, keep the switching lively!

FIRST EXECUTIONER

What's this? So there you are! God blast Toby, he's ratted on us! Oh, sir, go easy. Little did we dream things would turn out this way.

SECOND EXECUTIONER

Sir, sir, don't beat us any more! Our arms and legs are shattered as it is. We'll never again be any use to anybody. Bad cess to Toby's hide, he's been a traitor. Woe's us, alas!

THIRD EXECUTIONER

Lord, let me live! I beg your forgiveness for my lapse. May God's wrath light on that cursed boy, so fast of foot he got to you and brought disgrace to us.

TYRANT

Our account is now squared. But if I have to come and fetch you a second time, you can be sure of faring even better! Come with me at once to the forest.

A DEVIL

I cry peace to all, both the wild and the tame. I am Monfras,[86] never ashamed of doing my best to do my worst. I have a following, my zealous, fervent worshippers, who will come home to the fold at last.

SECOND DEVIL

Through your wiles and your enchantments you are a clever deceiver, but I am craftier still. Men call me Skirlywit, the slippery one. Whoever tries to match wits with me, faith, he gets as good in return.

FIRST DEVIL

Let us proceed to the temple where the tyrant is about to offer solemn rites of sacrifice that his sins may prosper. Let's take a peep at him, not that it's bound to be for his good.
(*Let him go down to the temple.*)

TYRANT

Come into the temple, sirs, one and all. This our god is no ordinary god. He is the kind who must be honored.
(*All kneel.*)
I offer up the head of a more or less white bull. Here it is, old boy. Catch!

FIRST EXECUTIONER

I'll not be haughty toward my god. Mohammed, take unto thyself this ram's head, its horns nicely gilded over. Don't be ashamed of my offering; only, since it's rather on the ripe side, I'm setting it nearer your nose than mine.

SECOND EXECUTIONER

To my god, I offer a horse's head. Receive it for your treasure room. A magnificent gift, it's furnished with wooden hooks to hang it by. It's worth several pence to a baby like you.

THIRD EXECUTIONER

To my god, the blessed Jove, I sacrifice three ravens with marvelously swollen crops. They are worth tuppence each. I fetched them only yesterday from the carcass of a dead horse on the moors.

MENIAL

To the presence of my god, Jove, I gladly offer a cat. A better mouser doesn't exist. I brought it in my bosom the day before

yesterday from Morvelys,[87] where the devil was anointed. Besides the cat, I offer a buck's head and a skinned goat. Now thank us, my god, for these offerings!
(All the executioners sing.)

DEVIL

I bless you with the left hand.[88] See to it that all your actions are evil in fact as well as intention, and do not neglect to rob the poor. Neighbors' curses are stepping-stones to success.

FIRST EXECUTIONER

Now that our Holy Father on the North[89] has given us his blessing and commanded us to rob the poor, let's be off.

SECOND EXECUTIONER

My arms itch from going so long without raising hell. Let's be on the move to find us a traitor or maybe a cheater we'd like to get our hands on.

THIRD EXECUTIONER

Makes no difference where we go. That we'll never come back is what our nearest and dearest pray for most often. But as for us, we grow merrier and merrier every day.

KING'S SECOND HUNTSMAN

Majesty, I warned you that a powerful tyrant has risen against you. Now there he is in the meadow. You can see him with his armed host.

KING

Let everyone arm himself. We would play a coward's part were we to fail to bear ourselves better than he. For this tyrant is an unbeliever, who likes to be forever riding out and making war.

Nevertheless, I shall first debate him to the very teeth, and then, if he prefers to fight, I shall drive a spear into his heart.
(To the battleground, with two streamers.)

TYRANT

Ho, sirs. What is the meaning of this array? Tell me straight out who gave you license to trespass on my domain to hunt the game reserved for lords? Answer me, on penalty of death!

KING

Tyrant, control yourself, sir! No one of your blood has ever yet been born the heir to this inheritance. Halt where you are and curb your impudence. I have been sovereign over this kingdom for twenty unbroken years.

TYRANT

So it's you, prince, is it, who have ventured to come here? You'd be better advised to ask my permission for leave to withdraw while there's still time, for if we come to blows, only one of us will go away laughing.

KING

Now by him whom Judas sold, I don't give one sterile bean for all your bluster. I am not your vassal nor have I ever done you feudal service for any reason whatsoever. And if you now presume to lay a spurious claim on me, before I leave you will be dealt with as you deserve.

TYRANT

Threaten me, would you? Get out of here, you lying, whoreson scum! You and your parcel of dirty whelps, go hang or I'll have your heart's blood soaking the grass before the sun goes down!

KING

That is something you are not powerful enough to accomplish, neither you nor any other infidel, defender of a false faith. By the Lord Christ of mercy, in my eyes you are just a dog! Renounce your evil creed or else it will be I who sheds your blood upon the green. Never attempt to threaten the followers of Christ.

TYRANT

I defy you and all your breed! Fie, fie a thousand times over on all

Christians! Do you renounce *your* faith. Otherwise, by Satan, you and all who are with you shall perish in agony.

KING

We will never forswear the Faith out of fear of you or any unbelieving Jew![90] I do not fear the test of upholding the Christian faith right here and now on this green plot. I am ready.

TYRANT

Charles, Beaumont, Hector,[91] go for them! To arms, to arms! May the devil himself be your chum when you die if you quit now. Seize the vermin for me. Down with the false and filthy Christians!

KING

You shall swing by your beards, traitors, before you are able to do that. Attack when you will, there are soldiers on hand and ready to respond in kind. Men-at-arms, have at them! May I never see your surrender to a Jew!
(Here they shall fight.)

KING

Woe, alas, we must retreat in haste, lest we perish. We are not strong enough this time. Some, indeed, have been captured by the graceless Jew. Oh, God, what is to happen now?
(Let him retire homeward.)

TYRANT

Heartiest congratulations, my most excellent soldiers! But tell me, out of all those who have run away, haven't we captured even one?

THIRD KNIGHT OF THE TYRANT

(Let him have seized the Woman's Son.)
Yes, here's one of their young men. I have just captured him, for which I ask your thanks, my lord.

TYRANT

May you prosper, my noble warrior! As for him, he shall pay his weight in gold before he's free, and shall, what's more, renounce his faith. Otherwise, he shall rot as a prisoner in the stocks.

SON

That is a thing I will not do. I will not deny Jesus Christ no matter what you are able to do to me. In spite of you, I shall continue to worship him who made the Feast Day and the First Day of the Week.

TYRANT

Very well, if you won't budge from allegiance to your god, off you go to prison. Ho, jailors, come here to me! Put this man in the dungeon. Unless and until he denies Christ, the son of Marian, there he shall rot.
(He goes up into his tower.)

JAILOR

We obey your command, my lord.
(To the Woman's Son)
Come with us, you, to be locked up. Seems you got a mite above yourself, didn't you, to go and rub our master the wrong way? You'll be sorry!

BOY

We'll shackle him so tight he won't be able to move hand or foot. Miserable you, a man bent on holding out. Here's where you'll wither away with nothing to eat, nothing to drink....

FIRST MESSENGER

(To the Son's Mother)
Greetings, good woman. I am the bearer of bad news. Your son has fallen into the hands of the tyrant and infidel. I grieve to say that I don't know what will happen to him.

WOMAN

Oh, what heart-break! Alas, he was my only child, my only

comfort in this world. I will go to Blessed Mary, whom I serve, and pray to her from the bottom of my aching heart for my son....
(Let her go over to the church of the Blessed Mary. She remains kneeling there.)

Mary, Virgin Mother, I can hold nothing back. Help my son and restore him to me. Mary, I have always served you as best I could. Blessed Mary, for my sake break his bonds. If it is your will, he would surely be set free.

TYRANT

Ho, jailors, listen to me! I order you, on pain of dismembering, to give neither food nor drink to that fellow I have committed to prison. Tomorrow, by my soul, I shall forthwith hang, draw, and quarter him.

JAILOR

(To the Tyrant)

Lord, your wish is our command. There'll be no banquets for him, that's a sure thing. In fact, if he's to be hanged tomorrow, I'm not one to waste food on him.

WOMAN

Mary, these many times have I prayed to you for my son, yet where is the gift of your consolation? Can it be that you are unmoved by my tears? If there is such a thing as mercy, why, Mary, won't you hear me this night?

Mary, I am left with no choice since to pray is useless. My son is in chains, Mary, listen and believe. In place of my precious child your little one shall go home with me today.

Mary, give me your Jesus from your arm. No matter what the peril or the sin, he shall come home with me this hour. Come, babe, come. Farewell to you, Mary, I'll no longer weary you with my pleading.
(Let her go away with the Jesus.)

Jesus, I wish you joy. I'll guard you ever so carefully as I would my own child.
(A coffer ready.)

I'll wrap you in fine linen and put you safely in my coffer and lock it. And now that I'm happier, I'll go to my bed.

MARY

(She speaks in heaven.)

Jesus, my beloved son, whose knowledge of all things is perfect and to whom all hearts are opened, I am moved to bring speedy help to my earthly servant.

JESUS

O Mother, ever do that which pleases you. Whoever bends the knee to you shall in due time be comforted. See to your servant in accordance with your purpose and desire.

(Mary goes down with two angels to the prison.)

MARY

How is it with you, young man? Surely you have suffered much in this place without deserving it. But to him who is in a state of grace, God's mercy shall not be lacking in the end.

SON

Jesus, Lord, come to my aid, for I can never save myself! The brightness dazzles me. As I hope to be loved, I cannot comprehend the splendor that surrounds me.

MARY

Be of good courage! Bear up! Though you are faint with weakness, you shall have strength. Do not lose heart, for I will free you from this prison. I have come for your good.

SON

O Cross of Christ! *Benedicite!* Who can have come to me here with all the doors fast shut? But a moment ago it was deep night, yet now there is a glory before me and the likeness of a woman, a queen surely, in the midst of it!

MARY

Stretch out your legs. I will draw the fetters off them and will open the doors for you. Keys are worthless to prevent me.

And now, my son, go to your mother and tell her that Mary has set you free. Also impress upon her that she is to bring back my Son to me and again serve me daily in the years to come.

SON

Mary, may your name be praised! I was not worthy of your guidance. Thank you, Mary, oh, thank you! Well I know that without your help, which I did not deserve, I would have perished.

MARY

My blessing go with you and with your mother. Tell her that although I may have seemed slow in giving heed to her prayers, it was never my wish to forget her.
(*Let Mary pass to heaven.*)

JAILOR

Out, we're in trouble! On your feet, mate. Everything's on fire, the prison's ablaze. I think a way out's been found.

BOY

The prisoner's gone right through the bolted doors! Who the devil's been here? Come on, let's go tell the tyrant....Oh, God damn it, here he comes, the bad egg himself!

JAILOR

(*To the Tyrant*)
Oh, sir. Trouble, sir, trouble. The prisoner has escaped only seconds ago. A great light went with him. By the God who made me, I've never been more frightened!

TYRANT

Out, woe's me! Blast it, oh, blast it! Where has my prisoner gone? If he's gotten clean away, by my soul, you're as good as dead. Those whoresons were drunk and let the country people set him free. I know it!

BOY

God curse you, master, slow down! There are those who claim
and without any swearing or forswearing neither, that it was Mary
herself who freed him, and that you're to blame for being so hard on
the poor.
(A stick ready.)

TYRANT

So that's how it is, eh? *Mal!* To hell with you! If you've a mind to
slander me, jabbering about how cruel I am, you're going to pay for
it, as God is my witness. Take that! I'll put a stop to your evil
tongue.
(He beats them.)

SON

Put your mind at ease, mother, and give reverent thanks to
Mary. It would be very wrong of us not to pay her homage. Most
fortunately for me, dear mother, she has delivered me from a
prison where I was being infamously treated.

WOMAN

Mary be praised! The sight of you, my son, lets me live again.
How were you freed? Dearest boy, please tell me.

SON

Mary came to me last night, came right into the prison with light
and a great sound. Truly, I'm not sure whether I was asleep or
awake. She loosed my chains and opened the door for me, gently
bidding me to go home to my mother.
"Tell your mother," she said, "that I have freed you, but let her
restore my Son to me. That is only right since now she has her
child."

WOMAN

Heartfelt thanks to Blessed Mary! Those she wishes to help will
not be disappointed in the end. Because she failed to give you back

to me, my heart was sick with anguish, and I took her child from her sacred image.

But now I will most gladly carry the child back to the image, going quickly into the church. See, here it is. I kept it safe for I never wanted to harm it....

Mary, joy to you. Mary, accept my deepest thanks for giving me my son again.

(She goes down to the church of the Blessed Mary with the Jesus.)

Mary, take your child. Mary, I have been too slack in my duty toward you. But even as I beg your forgiveness, I promise to be among your willing servants for evermore.

(Let her go home.)

LIFE OF MERIASEK (Part III)[92]

(A Madman and a Head of Family ready.)

MADMAN

(Twisting and lurching about)

I'll fix you, you tricksters! Why have you bound me? I'll break your lousy heads for you!

HEAD OF FAMILY

You can say it, but you can't do it. You're chained fast. I'm going to take you to Meriasek to see if you can be cured.

MADMAN

So tell me, goggle-eyes, what have I to do with Meriasek? May the devil roast you!...

HEAD OF FAMILY

A good day to you, Meriasek. I have this demented man with me here, and people have advised me that I should bring him to you for relief.[93]

MERIASEK

May the Lord Jesus in heaven help us all, the sick and the sound. This is a pitiful sight, a handsome young man burdened with chains.

MADMAN

In spite of my chains, if you'd just come a little closer, I'd scalp your shaved pate and break your legs for you at the same time!

MERIASEK

(He kneels.)

Lord Jesus, I beseech you to cure this man. Christ Jesus, gracious Lord, restore him to his right mind. Jesus, Lord, Virgin's Son, deliver him from the enemy within. Jesus, permit the granting of my plea and may Mary intercede on my behalf.

Stand still, good man. In the name of Mary's Son I set you free. Let us pray that He who is able, if such is his will, to cure without the need of earthly remedy, now heal you. Amen.

MADMAN

Glory to Christ Jesus and much honor to you, Meriasek. Through you, Christ has restored my sanity. It shall ever be my duty, Meriasek, to reverence, honor, and serve you for the rest of my life. *(He ends.)*

MERIASEK

I will return to my oratory, there to beseech Mary for her unceasing help in preserving me from temptation and from every evil thought....
(He kneels at the oratory.)

Jesus, most gracious Lord, yours is the glory and the triumph. Jesus, universal Lord, keep my body and soul from all defilement. Blessed Mary, virgin without spot, ever aid me in my hour of need. Mary, whom I adore, pray to God for my salvation.

JESUS

My dear angels, descend to the earth and give heavenly food to

106

Meriasek. He shall be nourished by my grace. His deeds are pleasing in my sight, and his name is everywhere blessed.

MICHAEL

Lord, your will be done. We shall hasten to his side, and he shall receive from our hands the perfect comfort of that nourishment whose only source is the Maker of All Things.
(They descend – organs[94] or singing.)

GABRIEL

Joy to you, Meriasek. Christ, our beloved Lord, has sent us to you for your comfort. However long your penitential fasts may run, you shall henceforth be sustained by celestial food.
(Taking food with praises, he feels himself refreshed from day to day by divine nourishment.)[95]

MERIASEK

(He kneels.)

May Jesus, Lord of heaven and earth, be forever glorified! Jesus Christ, he who faithfully serves you in this world shall never come to harm. Jesus, I give thanks for that I am fed with the food of heaven. I shall not fear, Lord, though I were to fast day after day.

EPISODE OF ST. SILVESTER (Part II)[96]

(Here a duke, that is, First Magician, shall parade.)

FIRST MAGICIAN DUKE

I am a peerless lord, a duke; likewise, an astrologer. As becomes a prince, I propose to go hunting with a sizable company in attendance. It has also been provided that the bishop will rendezvous with me.

SECOND MAGICIAN DUKE

We had better be wary. A large dragon is known to inhabit a

nearby cave. Were we to encounter it, we'd be dead, from first to last. Due caution is surely advisable.

HUNTSMAN TO THE DUKES

There are men-at-arms here, and archers, quite capable of dispatching it. My hounds alone, provided they are hungry enough, would doubtless tear it to pieces before they were through.
(He goes down with the men-at-arms.)

(Here the Bishop of Poli shall parade.)

BISHOP OF POLI

I am a bishop from head to toe, an outstanding prelate. A month ago, I agreed to meet the Magician Duke yonder at the edge of the meadows. I know him for an eminent personage, a man of wise counsel. Crozier-bearer, are you ready for my orders?

CROZIER-BEARER

Ready, my good lord. But here's a case of poor management. We can't have breakfast before setting out, yet I'm empty. Ah, God must have cursed the kitchen, the food and drink are so skimpy!
(They go down.)

BISHOP OF POLI

Greetings and salutations, noble duke, illustrious magician. I and my crozier-bearer diviner have come to join you for the hunt. Let us not, however, keep overmuch to the low ground of the valley, since it seems there is a dragon, a big one, hereabouts.

FIRST MAGICIAN DUKE

Welcome, father bishop. In my considered opinion, no dragon will venture to approach us. And if it should as much as come in sight, I'm confident there are assuredly enough people on hand to do away with it.
(Here the dragon ready on the platea.)

SECOND MAGICIAN DUKE

We must not trust to that. Lords, let us get away from here.

Come, there it is, no doubt about it. Out, it will kill us with its tongue of flame! A thousand armed men couldn't stand up to it! *(Here a gun*[97] *ready in the dragon's mouth, and fire.)*

FIRST DUKE

Ho, have at it! Let fly! Some have already been swallowed by the thing!
(Some of the soldiers swallowed.)
What the devil shall we do? May Mohammed hobble you! Look, it's voiding egg-like stool among us. See?

BISHOP OF POLI

Oh, woe, woe! Run or we're dead, by Mohammed, dead to the last man! Let us go to the Emperor Constantine and tell him that he is responsible for this.

(Here Constantine shall parade.)

FIRST DUKE

(To Constantine)
Hail, Emperor Constantine! To you, sire, we cry, "Out upon it!" The country is a shambles and many are dead because of you. The great, cave-dwelling dragon kills every man who dares to stand up to it. Such is the fact.

BISHOP OF POLI

Nothing has gone right in this country since you became a Christian. God's curse on him who converted you! I have yet to hear that anyone who worshipped the recreant Christ ever fared well.

CONSTANTINE

Lords, restrain yourselves. Christ and Mary, his mother, will come to our aid. Approach, messenger. Go at once and fetch Silvester, that I may speak to him.

MESSENGER

(To Constantine)
Peerless lord, I will bring Silvester to you within a day. No sleep

for my feet. I shall neither eat nor sleep until I address him face to face....
(To Silvester)

Silvester, joy to you! You must come to the Emperor immediately, for he wishes to speak to you as soon as possible.
(Silvester goes down.)

SILVESTER

I am always willing to attend Constantine at his command. He is a mighty sovereign....
(To Constantine)

Imperial sir, joy to you! Here am I, nor had I any wish to delay my coming.

CONSTANTINE

I hear that there is a dragon hereabouts which is killing uncounted numbers of people without hindrance. I am accused of being to blame as a result of my having received baptism.
(Constantine goes down.)

SILVESTER

Through the power of Christ, the Lord on high, I shall make the dragon so tame that it will do no further harm, to the end that all who are in Rome may learn that to give judgment is reserved to Jesus Christ alone in strict accordance with His Will.

FIRST MAGICIAN DUKE

Already and in a single day, by my faith, the dragon has slain a hundred men. If now you conquer it, we will turn to Christ. However, it is my feeling that you cannot do it.

SILVESTER

After I have prayed, I will go to meet the creature.
(He kneels.)

JESUS

Peter, betake yourself in my name to Silvester. Fully reassure him and tell him that he shall prevail against the dragon by my power. He has my love, and I shall not forget him.

PETER

Lord, I will do your bidding and will let Silvester know of it at once, so that he shall no longer fear the dragon. He shall lead it as if it were a pet lamb and, what is more, banish it far into the desert through God's might.
(Peter descends alone to Silvester on the platea.)
Rejoice, good Silvester! It is Christ's wish that you overcome the dragon. Take your two chaplains with you and help will come promptly.

SILVESTER

May the Lord of Heaven succor me. I do not know who comes thus to my aid, yet great is Christ's power and great my trust in His unfailing grace.

PETER

I am one of Christ's apostles, he whose rightful name is Peter. You need fear no deception in this matter....[98]
Say to the dragon: "In the name of Jesus Christ, Mary's Son, who was born of a pure virgin, who died upon the Cross, was buried in the Sepulchre, rose again on the third day, ascended into heaven whence on the Last Day he will surely come to judge us in the flesh — in His Name, dragon, come forth to me here!"
Take a cross with you, and you shall be able to lead the beast exactly as you please. Because you are his faithful servant, Jesus will be with you.

SILVESTER

May this hour be sanctified. I will hasten to confront the beast. Chaplains, come with me and in Mary's name bear aloft before us the emblem of the Cross.
(A cross ready for Silvester's First Chaplain.)

FIRST CHAPLAIN

While I bear the cross, let my fellow carry a lighted lantern. I

have heard that the monster's cave is hundreds of feet deep. Guard us, O Christ, against the perils of the dark.
(Second Chaplain bears the lantern.)

FIRST MAGICIAN DUKE

Sirs, let us go and see what Silvester can do to make an end of the great dragon. I don't believe he can manage anything, in fact, beyond fooling us with a bit of magic.

SILVESTER

(He kneels.)
In the name of Christ Jesus, Mary's Son, who was dead and buried, rose again on the third day, ascended to heaven and to the right hand of God the Father, and who shall come on the Day of Doom to judge the good and the bad, come out in obedience to Christ's command as it was entrusted to me here on earth!
(The dragon comes forth from the cave.)

FIRST MAGICIAN DUKE

Here it comes! We'd best get back. Out, out, its fecal blast overwhelms me, never more to rise!
(He falls to the ground and dies.)

SECOND MAGICIAN DUKE

I am slain by its wind! Precious Mohammed, saint of saints,[99] there is no escape for me. Would that I'd looked out for myself sooner. This is a hideous end.
(He falls to the ground and dies.)

SILVESTER

Halt, dragon, and be still. I shall lay hold of you in the name of the beloved Christ and through God's power lead you like a lamb — thus.

CONSTANTINE

All honor to you, Silvester! You have proved past doubt that Christ is Lord of Lords. I had need of that proof. What do you say, sirs? Is this not a holy man?

112

BISHOP OF POLI

There are still these dead men here. If they could be brought back to life, each of us, regardless of rank, would have reason to believe in Jesus the son of Mary.

SILVESTER

Jesus, lord of all, grant that these who now lie slain may arise, restored to life and health. And if they are wise, they will henceforth sin no more.
(All, including the two dukes, arise.)

FIRST MAGICIAN DUKE

Silvester, may your name be honored! From this day forward, I will believe in Christ, the God of mercy. I will obtain baptism and worship the son of Mary. As for the dragon, it is an evil beast.

SECOND MAGICIAN DUKE

Restored to my senses, I, too, will receive baptism and worship Jesus forever. The dragon I have no wish to see. With its false and wicked face, the face of a reptile, it is a devilish creature!

SILVESTER

You need have no fear of that. By the grace of Jesus on high, I will send it into the desert where it can do no harm. In the name of the merciful Christ, I command you, dragon, make haste into the wilderness. Begone! And see to it that you never harm either man or beast, either weak or strong, nor ever return again, evil thing that you are, on pain of death.[100]

BISHOP OF POLI

Beyond a shadow of doubt, it is gone. All Rome is eternally in your debt, Silvester. Pray baptize us forthwith. Here it has been clearly shown that there is no God save Jesus Christ, ever glorious.
(Holy water ready.)

SILVESTER

I will baptize you together here and now before we part: *In nomine Patris et Filii et Spiritus Sancti Amen.*

Now, my clergy, let us go to my palace without delay.

SECOND CHAPLAIN

We are ready to accompany you, Silvester, rare as are the opportunities for us to serve you. Glory be to Christ, in that through you so many souls have been saved here today!

CONSTANTINE

Glory be to Christ Our Savior. Through Silvester the people of Rome have been delivered this day from a double death. First, many souls have been converted from paganism to the one true way. Second, all of us have been rescued outright from that hellish serpent, the dragon.

Let us all accompany Silvester in procession to his court. Who among us is not his debtor? Were it not for him, many of us would surely have been devoured by the merciless beast.
(*They go in procession to the Pope's palace.*)

LIFE OF MERIASEK (Part IV)[101]

A CRIPPLE

Oh, God, how great is my affliction, arms and legs crippled from shoulder to finger, from hip to toe! I can walk only on crutches. How weak I am, how diseased. Although I have no idea when I shall find him, I am making my way to Meriasek.

I have spent the livelong night in the cold and wretchedness of the open while many sleep under shelter. Constantly slipping into puddles, the flesh of my knees scraped to the bone, there is no hope of getting to my feet....

Have I come at last to the right place? God bless you, good man. For the love of sweet Jesus, can you, out of kindness, tell me where I might find Meriasek?

MERIASEK

You are speaking to him. Tell me of your need without delay, for it is always my desire to help the poor and unfortunate in this world.

114

CRIPPLE

I am a cripple, riddled with sores, now come to you, thank God, in my dire need. For the sake of the Passion which Jesus bore for us, restore me to health.

All my limbs are crippled, yet Death shuns me. If I am to get about, I must crawl. Few are minded so much as to come in sight of me, let alone approach and look on me. Here I am, naked as a beast, creeping along the ground.

MERIASEK

(He kneels.)

Humbly I pray that Jesus, maker of heaven and earth, will give you health, making it possible for you to get about freely, even as He is able, by spiritual power alone, to banish all disease and pain from your limbs.

May Jesus Christ Our Savior raise you up from off the ground. May Mary come to your aid, and if it be her will, now grant you health.

CRIPPLE

How great my joy, O Lord! I give thanks to Christ, the merciful, and to you, Meriasek. My limbs are straight and strong again. I can walk with confidence and am completely healed!

MERIASEK

Thanks be to Jesus! Here are clothes to cover your nakedness, good man; likewise, food and drink. Give your thanks to Christ and his power. It is He who is truly your physician.

CRIPPLE

May Jesus in heaven, the glorious, virgin-born Son, reward you, Meriasek, ever prepared to help the poor.

MERIASEK

(He lies in the oratory.)[102]

Gather around me, my brethren. I have received the Body of my Lord this day, as is my duty. The time has come when we must part,

115

however beautiful our fellowship has been.

Thanks be to Jesus, death has touched me, and I must leave this world. Brethren, study to be kind and never fail to relieve the poor.

DEAN

(To Meriasek)
What will become of us, my lord, if you depart from us? I know past doubt that we shall never again have a lord like you.

MERIASEK

The hour is near. I thank Christ for His goodness to me in this life. Shriven, houseled, aneled, I give thanks to Jesus. To God the Father and to Christ, true Son of the Virgin, I will pray for all those who serve me in this world.
(He kneels.)
Whosoever shall honor me on earth, grant them, Jesus, Lord, the privilege of confession before they die and to receive Christ's Body and therewith the holy oil, that their souls may enter into the bliss of the Kingdom of Heaven.

Wheresoever I might be honored, I pray that my petitioners may enjoy the fullness of health and freedom from all sickness, whether of the body or the soul, and that they may have food and the means necessary to support life.

In Cornwall I shall have a house of worship nearby to Mary of Camborne.[103] I will gladly ease the burdens of those who come to seek me there, even though my body lie elsewhere. Whoever prays in that place shall be heard by Jesus and his petition granted, provided it be lawful.

My Feast Day shall be appointed for the first Friday of June in perpetuity. I ask that the blessing of Christ, Lord of the Saints, and likewise my own blessing remain forever upon those who keep my Feast.

A CANON

How are you now, Meriasek? Though you seem to have grown considerably weaker, be of good cheer. It is we who may well be the ones to pine after you, full of longing for you if you were to leave us.

116

MERIASEK

On a Friday, Christ Jesus, our treasure, died for us. On a Friday, I am glad to yield up my soul to my Savior. On a Friday, therefore, let my children faithfully keep my Feast forevermore.

Brethren, come nearer now. As a token of love, I will kiss each of you in the name of Mary's Son. Let us part in submission.

In manus tuas, Domine, spiritum meum commendo.
(And so he sent forth his spirit.)[104]

JESUS

Fly to earth, my angels, and very gently bring the soul of Meriasek to me. All that he asked for on earth is granted. His was a life of goodness and beauty.

MICHAEL

Lord, he has won his place in heaven through faithful service to you. As is our rightful duty, we will do your bidding with all speed.

GABRIEL

Rejoice, Meriasek! All your petitions have been granted and in happiness you shall go to heaven, there to abide in unending bliss.

BISHOP OF CORNOUAILLE

My crozier-bearer, it has come to my ears that Meriasek is at the point of death. I wish to go to him to learn whether he yet lives or has died. During my lifetime, I do not expect to see his like again in Brittany.

(He goes down.)

COUNT OF VANNES

I mourn the news that Meriasek now lies upon his bier. Come with me, knights. We will go at once that we may lay him in the earth.

(They go down.)[105]

SECOND BISHOP

The lords are on their way to Meriasek's burial. God watch over

his soul. Surely there will not be another like him in Brittany.
(He goes down.)

COUNT OF VANNES

Greetings, lords. I have been informed that the noble Meriasek
has passed away. I assume that you proceed to his funeral as do we.

BISHOP OF CORNOUAILLE

Sir Count, we do, indeed. Even as he was a most worthy man, it is
our obligation to go and reverently lay him in earth. He was
Christ's faithful servant.
(Count Globus goes down.)

SECOND BISHOP

Joy to you, and grace. I am gratified by the sight of this company.
For as much as Meriasek has departed this life, may Jesus, mighty
Lord, grant bliss to his soul.

COUNT GLOBUS

He was truly a rare soul from his first breath, every Breton
knows that, and even rarer in what he was able to accomplish. I
have personally experienced a demonstration of his power.

For many years I was blind. No physician could be found who
was able to restore my sight. But when I eventually came to
Meriasek, by the grace of Christ, the King of Heaven, he gave me
back my sight. For him, thanks be to Jesus, the cure was easy.

BISHOP OF CORNOUAILLE

Many a man in this world is indebted to Meriasek and owes him
unceasing veneration. I have complete faith that after his labors
here he is now a saint in heaven.

COUNT OF VANNES

(To the Dean)

God save the chapter![106] Dean and sir, has Meriasek died? It is
widely rumored that his soul has gone from this world, as I am
persuaded, to bliss.

DEAN

My lord, he has departed this life. I believe that his soul is with the Godhead. No man, to my knowledge, has ever made a more beauteous end, by my faith.

CANON

It was on Friday morning that he said Mass, said it indeed perfectly and gloriously. Then he told us that thanks to mighty Jesus he had felt death touch him.
(The procession ready, and two censers.)

DEAN

He petitioned Christ in behalf of those who might in future honor his life's work. Then he called us to him and bade us receive his kiss. He lifted up his hands, beseeching God's mercy, and we saw him raise his happy eyes toward heaven. The verse *In manus tuas* came from his lips without a falter and when it was ended, he yielded up his soul to the abounding grace of God the Father.

CANON

Most people are not aware of the real nature of his daily life. Although the stuff of his outer garment was usually of good quality, he always wore a hair shirt next his skin.[107] At night his covering was not blankets or sheets, just rough straw, and such sleep as he allowed himself was never long.

DEAN

In his worship of Christ, he was much like John the Baptist. He took neither wine nor cider. Through the hours of darkness he would kneel in worship a thousand times,[108] and in the day, likewise, he would go right down on both knees a thousand times in spite of the pain when they became so swollen he could scarcely walk save in a crouch.

CANON

He was always in the church, reading or at prayer. He spoke nothing but good. He must have been fed with manna from heaven,[109] for otherwise, in good faith, I do not see how he could have kept body and soul together.

COUNT OF VANNES

How great a loss this surely is for all of us in Brittany. And now, masters, if you are ready, we shall proceed to church for the burial.

DEAN

Everything is ready here. The chapter is assembled in due order as is seemly toward an illustrious man. The people also are gathering fast. He was loved beyond considerations of rank by young and old.

COUNT OF VANNES

He deserved that love. Many were the ailing who obtained relief from him: the blind and the deaf, cripples, paralytics, and a variety of other sufferers too many to be counted.

DEAN

Let us move forward, invoking the name of God and of Mary, Mother of Jesus. Pray assist us with the bier that we may enter the church. Christ grant us ever to do that which is good.

COUNT OF VANNES

I will carry the one end. I don't believe I have ever loved a man more. He was utterly filled with goodness and with blessedness as well. Happy the day that he was born!

COUNT GLOBUS

I will carry the other end. Meriasek cured my blindness. May his name never cease to be venerated even as I shall honor it for the rest of my life....

DEAN

Let the clergy now raise their voices in the name of God's mercy, and let us not pause on our way to the graveside. Beyond doubt, this man deserved the country's homage.

(Here they sing.)[110]

SECOND BISHOP

Prepare the grave in all seemliness that we may bury him, in Christ's name, as is our debt to one so highly esteemed. His good deeds were manifold, thanks be to Jesus.

NAKED MAN

We have dug the grave. When I was a cripple and a leper, he healed me. I owe him service in this world and devotion.

CRIPPLE

We have cleaned the grave. It awaits your pleasure, my lords. Ah, God, how grieved we are to see the body of Meriasek go into the ground.

BISHOP OF CORNOUAILLE

We cannot oppose God's will. In His name, therefore, lay the body in the grave, and I will pronounce the Benediction in the name of my Lord Jesus.

COUNT OF VANNES

I now lay the body in the grave. Help me with it, Globus. Look upon the corpse outstretched. However great our earthly dominion, we shall all come to this.

BISHOP OF CORNOUAILLE

May the Lord of Heaven bless him. Now cover him with earth, my children, in God's name, and let us return home. Sorrow burdens me and many another here today.

COUNT OF VANNES

The peace of God be with all who are gathered here. Yesterday and today we have presented the life of Meriasek. The petitions of those who have put their trust in him and earnestly entreated him in their prayers, Jesus has assuredly granted.

The blessing of Meriasek, of beloved Mary of Camborne, and of the Apostles go with you. Before you leave, we urge you to take something to drink for the benefit of the play.

Now, pipers, blow, and let everybody join the dancing. Go home if you must, but if you can stay on, you'll be welcome though you were with us for a week![111]

Finitur per dominum HADTON anno domine Mlvciiij.[112]

NOTES

All line references conform to the numbering of the Whitley Stokes edition of the play (London, 1872).

1. In the MS, the full heading of the play is HIC INCIPIT ORDINALE DE VITA SANCTI MEREADOCI EPISCOPI ET CONFESSORIS 'Here Begins the Play of the Life of Saint Meriasek, Bishop and Confessor.' The ritualistic flavor of the Latin, regularly employed for headings and stage-directions in the surviving Cornish drama of the Middle Ages, is reinforced by the term *ordinale*, a medieval Latin word suggesting in this context not only a rhetorical concept ('sequence of action,' 'order of progress') but also something ordained to be read or heard and likewise received in the spirit of religious devotion and edification.

The Cornish title by which the play is routinely identified is *Beunans Meriasek* (Life of Meriasek).

I have supplied the designation Part I (first of four parts or extended passages focused upon the days and ways of Meriasek himself) as a matter of convenience for the reader, who might otherwise become confused or irritated or both by the freedom with which the play temporarily abandons one line of action in order to pursue another, only to return to the previously established strand and carry on with it anew (see Introduction, *Beunans Meriasek* as Drama, for further comment on the play's structural characteristics).

2. Having been informed by this opening speech that Meriasek's father ranks as Duke of Brittany, we learn from the messenger at 1. 84 that the duke's name is Conan, a name prominent in both Wales and Brittany during the Middle Ages. History, as distinguished from legend, records how Conan of

123

Rennes took first place among rival Breton chiefs in the second half of the 10th c. and how his son, Geoffrey, assumed the title of duke. The Conan line apparently died out in the 12th c. but not before it had played a part in successfully opposing William the Conqueror's attempt to add much of Brittany to his domain.

That there were Conans among the medieval dukes of Brittany while that predominantly Celtic enclave enjoyed autonomy, if not outright independence, under the Frankish kings, is an established fact. The same cannot be affirmed of Meriasek's supposed familial connection with the Breton Conans. That connection, like so much pertaining to the saint, belongs to legend.

3. See n. 7 below.

4. The MS reads *bonilapper*, a probable coinage in a stanza whose meter is somewhat irregular and whose tone seems patently derisive. The original editor and translator, Whitley Stokes, gives up altogether on finding an English equivalent, resorting to an ellipsis and question mark. The late Morton Nance in his Unified Version with Amended Translation (typescript, Cornwall County Museum) turns to *bainne clabair* 'bonny clabber,' the Irish for curdled milk, adding that such a meaning "seems unlikely here." Viewed as a mildly satiric allusion to alma mater, Nance's gloss is not, however, without point. Other possible interpretations based on Fr. *bon* combined with M.E. *lapper* (borrowings from Old French and Middle English are a feature of the Cornish original) range from something as straightforward as 'lusty imbiber,' 'guzzler,' which at least has the virtue of being in harmony with the context, to sexual innuendoes which are not.

5. A predilection reminiscent of Chaucer's Summoner — which is not to say, of course, that the author(s) had acquaintance with him.

6. A reference to the horn-book, perhaps the earliest of visual aids to learning the alphabet. In his article "The Criss-Cross Row" (*Old Cornwall,* vol. 1, no. 5, 1927), Morton Nance wrote in part: "The horn-book...was for centuries down to about 1830 every child's first 'book.' This was an oaken battledore on which a sheet of paper containing the first reading lesson was held by a transparent plate of horn tacked down with strips of metal at its edges, the horn protecting the page from fingering. The handle by which it was held had also a hole for a string by which it could be hung on a nail or at the wrist of a child, as one sometimes sees it in pictures. In this, even in the 19th century, the cross was still prefixed to the alphabet, and the first step on the path of learning was to say, not 'A,' but 'Criss-cross,' a contraction of 'Christ's Cross'....In Thomas Morley's *Introduction to Music*, 1597, we find the alphabet rhymed as a first singing lesson for little choirboys, in which music and learning might begin together, thus:—

> 'Christes crosse be my speede
> In all vertue to proceede
> A.B.C.D.E.F.G....'"

7. Modern historians do not name a Conan among the medieval Breton chiefs traditionally accorded the title of king, such as Nominoë or Salamon. They tend to agree, however, that in the interests of establishing their native leadership in early Brittany as having existed well before the rise to farflung

124

hegemony of Clovis, king of the Franks (d. 511), the house of Conan and also that of Rohan (see n. 8) encouraged the legend of Conan Meriadoc (Meriasek), claiming him as a common ancestor.

According to Geoffrey of Monmouth's version of the legend (*History of the Kings of Britain*, Bk. 5, Sec. 12), Maximian, having invaded what is now Brittany and overrun it, bestows his conquest upon his military associate, Conan Meriadoc, saying (Sebastian Evans translation): "...in this kingdom will I make thee King, and it shall be another Britain that we will replenish with men of our own race...." Speaking through Maximian (a misnomer for Magnus Maximus, emperor from 383 to 388), Geoffrey means by "our own race" primarily his Welsh countrymen and the Cornish.

In naming a Conan as king of Brittany, the author of *Beunans Meriasek* is obviously in accord with legend, not only as he could have found it in Geoffrey's History, completed *c.* 1139, but also available to him in one or another hagiographical account of the saint's life and works in the liturgical books used in Brittany during the Middle Ages. For example, the first lesson of the second nocturn of Matins on the feast day of 'Saint Meriadec' in the Proper of Vannes commences as follows (G. H. Doble translation): "I. Meriadocus, who belonged to the illustrious stock of Conan, king of Lesser Britain, devoted himself from a child to the pursuit of all the virtues....."

The respect in which the playwright departs from all his potential sources, historical and legendary, consists of making King Conan not an ancestor of the young Meriasek but his contemporary. He thus compresses within the span of one normal lifetime what would presumably have required the passage of centuries: at a minimum from the latter half of the 4th c., the indicated time of Geoffrey's Conan Meriadoc, to the latter half of the 6th c. (*c.* 578), earliest suggested date for the birth of Meriasek by the Bollandist correction of Albert Le Grand's Life of St. Mériadec.

8. Although this proposed alliance is destined to come to nothing within the world of *Beunans Meriasek*, in the world of historical fact Conan III of Brittany did marry Matilda, the illegitimate daughter of Henry I, king of England from 1100 to 1135. Moreover, Conan III's granddaughter, Constance, is said to have married a Rohan, member of the second prominent Breton family, along with the house of Conan, to which the play is at pains to relate Meriasek by ties of blood. The Rohan kinship comes to light when Meriasek assumes the life of a hermit at an isolated spot near Pontivy, down to modern times a family seat of the Rohans. The private chapel of Pontivy castle is dedicated to St. Meriasek.

9. A visitor from beyond the eastern border of both medieval and present-day Brittany.

10. *Luke* 18: 29-30.

11. Vulgate, *Luke* 16: 19-31, beginning *Homo quidam erat dives* 'There was a certain rich man....'

12. Historical district of southwestern Brittany with an extensive Atlantic coastline. The name is generally taken as derived from the Cornish (and Welsh) émigrés who fled Britain between the 5th and 7th centuries under pressure from

the encroaching Angles and Saxons, though the migration may have begun a century or so earlier.

13. Moved down from its MS position between ll. 510-511 for better continuity.

14. The southwestern tip of the Cornish peninsula. It lies approximately due north across the English Channel from the port of Brest.

15. The play is following local tradition in providing that Meriasek, newly arrived in Cornwall from Brittany, should find at Camborne a chapel dedicated to the Virgin. It is also a local tradition that this chapel once stood within the precincts of the town churchyard not far from the location of the present Camborne parish church. Aside from a scattering of old worked stones, whose conformations seem alien to any known reconstruction of the parish church or the onetime parish hall (alms house) nearby, the last remnants of which were removed as recently as 1954 (see Charles Thomas, *Christian Antiquities of Camborne*, p. 56), the archeological evidence for a Mary chapel separate from and perhaps antecedent to Camborne parish church is nil. The church is considered to date from the 12th c. at the earliest (Thomas, *op. cit.*, p. 137).

The earliest and least ambiguous item of documentary evidence for the existence of a Mary chapel at Camborne is dated 7 November 1435. It consists of an entry in the Episcopal Registers of the Diocese of Exeter (Lacy I. 316) under the terms of which Bishop Lacy granted an indulgence of 40 days to all persons visiting or contributing to the support of the free chapel of the Blessed Virgin Mary and St. Anne in the parish of Camborne.

16. Although at this point (ll. 652-54) Meriasek reaffirms his wish (ll. 637-40) to establish an oratory "linked with a house of Mary," the subsequent action of the play does not provide for his actually doing so. It does, however, leave intact the inference that in course of time a house of God that could rightfully be termed a church (Cor. *eglos*) would come into being at Meriasek's chosen place (Cor. *plas*).

17. A natural spring, with or without a small sheltering chapel, was for centuries a well-known landmark lying, as the play specifies (l. 664), in what was once an open meadow situated roughly northeast of Camborne parish church. Originally looked upon as a holy well and duly visited by the faithful on St. Meriasek's Feast Day, the first Friday in June (ll. 4302-05), it appears in later times to have become gradually secularized into a wishing well patronized for the most part by Camborne's younger generation. Finally, before the middle of the 19th c., we have the record of an eye-witness (see Thomas, *op. cit.*, p. 125), who says of the well on the Saint's name-day, "No one could pass up the street (now Tehidy Road, Camborne) without having a pitcher of water thrown at him."

Probably drained dry by mining operations near the middle of the last century, the once celebrated well is now commemorated, almost as an afterthought, on a bronze plaque which marks the starting-point of the first run of Richard Trevithick's road locomotive in 1801. The postscript reads: "Also near this spot was the once famous Well of St. Meriadoc supposed to possess healing qualities of great virtue." By tradition, those healing properties were directed against headache, deafness, and insanity as understood in the Middle Ages, *i.e.*, demonic possession.

18. Camborne is situated in the formerly very active tin-mining region of western Cornwall, about 3 miles inland from the sea on the north and an equal distance from Redruth to the east. The two communities were combined during the early 1930's into a single urban district which forms Cornwall's largest centre of population today (in excess of 30,000). Two centuries ago, the recorded population of Camborne parish as a whole was less than 3,000. Some four centuries ago, the 16th c. topographer and surveyor, John Norden (1548-1625?) described Camborne as follows: "A churche standing among the barayne hills." (*Speculi Britannie Pars: A Topographical and Historical Description of Cornwall*, not published until 1728).

19. According to the language of MS (ll. 720-26), Meriasek now proceeds to do something more than express the wish to make for himself an oratory (see n. 16) near Mary of Camborne's chapel. He chooses the site of what is envisioned as a full church (*eglos*) at the same location and anticipates its construction. Before returning to Brittany, he will confirm his act of establishment and bestow upon the place his blessing on the eve of departure for the Continent (ll. 990-1016). The play thus reinforces the local tradition that the prospective *eglos* actually became Camborne parish church and that St. Meriasek was its original patron rather than St. Martin of Tours, who was to rival Meriasek in time to come. The earliest known documentary confirmation of the church's dedication to Meriasek is found in the Episcopal Registers of Exeter (Grandisson I. 42) for the year 1329, where the church is referred to as *Ecclesia sancti Meriadoci de Cambron*. For a full discussion of the subject, see Thomas, *op. cit.*, pp. 21-22.

20. Syrian captain cured of leprosy by Elisha (II *Kings* 5: 1-14).

21. Under Cornish auspices, Teudar (Theodore, Theodoric) figures as a traditional villain. In the *Vita Petroci* (Life of Patrick) he is described as a man addicted to the infliction of cruel and unusual punishments. In *Vita Guigneri* (Life of Gwinear) and the *Life of St. Kea*, he appears as a persecutor of holy men. For a consideration of Teudar under other than Cornish auspices, see John Morris, *The Age of Arthur*, pp. 130-32.

Writing of Teudar, the late Henry Jenner (MS lecture, Cornwall County Museum, p. 22) suggested that the play's identification of the name, Teudar, with the role of tyrant was a "sly hit" at Britain's first Tudor king, Henry VII, whose imposition of heavy fines upon the Cornish in connection with the Perkin Warbeck rebellion must have occasioned resentment in early 16th c. Cornwall. Jenner's proposal is, of course, possible, particularly if it is limited to the idea that a turn-of-the-century Cornish audience may have been inclined to merge the traditional tyrant and their reigning sovereign in the one name. But if Jenner's suggestion is more ambitiously interpreted to mean that the role of Teudar was deliberately manipulated to satirize a locally unpopular monarch, possibility becomes strained because of the time factor alone. Henry VII did not ascend the throne until 1485; the Warbeck rebellion did not enter its Cornish phase until 1497. It is true that the surviving MS of the play is dated 1504 (see Introduction, Author and Date of Composition, and n. 112), but it by no means follows from this that 1504 is the date of the play's original composition, whether in part or as a whole. It is much more likely that one or another episode of *Meriasek* or, for that matter, much of it was written not only before Perkin Warbeck made his bid for the throne but also before Henry VII ascended it.

Through Rhys ap Teudar (Rhys, son of Teudar), the Cornish tyrant may be connected with a prominent Welshman of the 11th c., whose legendary conflict with his kinsmen, Conan/Meriadoc, may conceivably lie behind the names of Conan and Meriasek, as well as that of Teudar, in the play.

22. To a medieval Cornish audience, it would have mattered little that Teudar avows himself to be a follower of Mohammed; still less, perhaps, that he shows himself so ignorant of his faith or so indifferent to it that he fails to distinguish between Allah, the one God of Islam, and Mohammed, his Prophet among men. What would have mattered to the audience is that Teudar is not a Christian. Since he therefore falls in that broad category beyond the pale, the pagan category, there is no obligation upon a Christian playwright addressing an audience of fellow Christians to be scrupulous toward even the paramount articles of an alien creed.

In medieval Cornwall, as elsewhere in Britain, the experience of the Crusades may have contributed to the recognition-value of Mohammed's name as popularly synonymous with heathenism. To Cornish drama as represented by *Beunans Meriasek* and its far larger predecessor, the *Ordinalia*, Mohammed (*Mahound*) is no stranger, but of Allah there is not a single mention.

23. A conspicuous natural landmark in the form of a granite-topped hill with an elevation of about 750 feet. As Teudar's messenger states, Carn Brea (Cor. *carn bre* 'rocky hill') lies a short distance, less than 3 miles, east and slightly north of Camborne in Penwith Hundred. Penwith is the County of Cornwall's most westerly sub-division, characterized as a hundred by virtue of having a law court of its own.

24. Cure of insanity receives special emphasis in the cult of Meriasek. In Cornwall, the water of his Holy Well was regarded as a specific (see n. 17). At Stival in Brittany a handbell said to have belonged to the saint is preserved as a remedy for such maladies as headache and deafness. According to the late Canon G. H. Doble ("Saint Meriadoc," *The Saints of Cornwall*, Part I, p. 129), the procedure at Stival consisted of placing the bell "upon the head of persons suffering from headache and deafness and (making it) ring." The homeopathic principle is evident here.

In modern terminology, the tertian fever mentioned by Meriasek earlier in the same speech is a form of malaria, whose attacks of fever and chills recur every other day or, when considered inclusively, every third (tertian) day.

25. Specific identification of the rock traditionally known as Meriasek's Rock (*Carrek Veryasek*) is no longer possible. But such circumstantial factors as size, conformation, and location point to a "carn" now called Reens Rock in the immediate vicinity of Troon. Reens Rock is a large, isolated mass of granite providing a number of sheltered spaces in which a person might hide (children still do). It is situated approximately a mile and a half southeast of Camborne

parish church, not far from "the early trackway southwards from Camborne to the Channel coast" (Thomas, *op. cit.*, p. 36).

26. Both Stokes and Nance render this proper name 'Apollo,' a rendering which is consonant with the speaker, pagan Teudar, and the qualifying adjective he employs, Cor. *splan*, meaning bright, shining, splendid, glorious. The MS spelling, however, which reads *appolyn* (1. 1059) admits of a different and comparably plausible identification of the god not with Apollo but rather with Apollyon, the Greek form of the Hebraic name Abaddon (Heb. 'destruction') as it appears in *Rev*. 9:11. Since the name Apollyon may properly be viewed as one of the many equivalents for Satan, in its turn equivalent to Lucifer 'light-bearer,' we are again within the ambience of post-Homeric Phoebus Apollo (Phoebus, the bright or pure). The New Testament demon, Apollyon, would appear to have as much negative significance for the Christian and probably clerical author of *Meriasek* as would classical Apollo, if not more.

27. According to Nance, the Hobbyhorse, which had a spoon in its mouth for contributions, functioned as a kind of collection agent at medieval Cornwall's May Games. Teudar's local allusion, although loosely and ironically applied, seems to mean that those who play games must expect to pay for them.

28. Castle Pontivy (MS *pontelyne*) is not, like its Cornish name, an invention by the playwright. Now a tourist attraction located in the older section of Pontivy, central Brittany, it is said to have been built by Jean II de Rohan and dates from the 15th c. Its present facade is flanked by a pair of good-sized towers. The outer walls, surrounded by a moat, are 64 feet high. The castle's private chapel is dedicated to St. Meriasek whose kinsmen, according to the Breton portions of the play, were the highly-placed Rohans (see n. 8) as well as the princely house of Conan.

The river which passes through the town is the Blavet, misnamed Josselin in the play perhaps because a community bearing the latter name, situated on the river Oust only some 20 miles to the southeast of Pontivy, is the site of another Rohan stronghold, Castle Josselin, a fortress-mansion erected at least in part by Jean II, the presumptive builder of Castle Pontivy. The MS coinage, *pontelyne*, may represent a combination of Pontivy and Josselin, accidental or for purposes of rhyme.

29. Meriasek's mountain, measuring "a thousand paces from its base to its summit," accords well enough with his ascetic zeal as an anchorite but squares with neither the topography of Pontivy and its immediate environs nor with the Latin Life (*Vita Meriadoci*) which has been put forward as a documentary source for the play (see Introduction). The higher elevations near Quelven to the southwest of Pontivy, even supposing the playwright to have been aware of them, seem too remote from Castle Pontivy to be described as 'hard by the castle' *ryb an castel* (l. 1138). As for the *Vita*, it says only that Meriasek established his oratory *juxta castrum de ponte ivii distantem per mille passus* 'a thousand paces from Castle Pontivy.'

30. The designation Part I has been supplied to indicate the first of two episodes in the play devoted to Constantine the Great and Pope Silvester I.

31. Flavius Valerius Constantinus, Roman emperor, 306-337. From his initial base of power in Gaul and Britain, he crossed the Alps and marched upon Rome, defeating his rival, Maxentius, at the battle of the Milvian Bridge over the Tiber near Rome in 312, traditionally the year of his conversion to Christianity. As emperor in the West (Britain, Gaul, Italy), Constantine defeated and deposed Licinius, emperor in the East, thus becoming sole ruler of the Roman Empire in the year 324.

The Cornish audience responded, very likely, less to this character as Roman emperor than to his mere name, familiar in Celtic tradition though varying in status and connotation. A Saint Constantine, of whom almost nothing is now known, gave his name to a parish very near the Lizard, base of Teudar and only a few miles from Camborne.

32. An ancient sun-god of Mesopotamian origin said to have been imported into Roman religion by the emperor Heliogabulus (reigned 218-22) under the name of Sol Invictus, the Unconquerable (Unconquered) Sun. Heliogabulus or Elagabulus had been a priest of Sol Invictus before his choice as emperor by the Roman army in Syria. Constantine's invocation of Sol is as appropriate as the naming of Mohammed is inappropriate (see n.22). Constantine died in 337; Mohammed was born c. 570.

33. In his 1872 edition of *Beunans Meriasek,* Whitley Stokes construes MS *apol* (l. 1236) as a reference to Apollo, his translation of the whole line reading "In this world Apollo is made." Even if we accept the Stokes interpretation, which tends to disregard the rationale of the stanza, the presence of the word *devle* 'devil' in the immediate context of the preceding line (1235) suggests the demon Apollyon (see n. 26) rather than Apollo, one of whose principal associations is with clarity and light. The phrasal meaning of *apol* (a-*pol*) being 'of/from mud,' while its referent in the same line (1236) is *bysma* 'this earth,' 'this world,' rather strongly recommends the later Morton Nance translation (typescript, Cornwall County Museum): "In this world that is made of mud." I have chosen 'clay' over 'mud' for the sake of its Biblical flavor in the Authorized Version of 1611.

34. For an earlier and far more climatic employment of this metaphor in Cornish drama, see the second play, *Passio Christi,* of the *Ordinalia* trilogy as found in Edwin Norris, *The Ancient Cornish Drama* (1859), ll. 2925-27; Markham Harris, *The Cornish Ordinalia* (1969), Christ's Passion, p. 167 and p. 263, n. 19.

35. See Introduction for comment on the dramatic treatment of the characters labeled a Native (*Domesticus*) or a Menial (*Calo*), in all but one instance anonymous yet not featureless creations (see n. 83).

36. Sometimes listed as the first of the medieval popes, Silvester I reigned from 314 to 335. He was thus a contemporary of Constantine the Great, representing one of the rare instances whereby the highly elastic chronology of the play can be reconciled with history. His papacy undoubtedly fell heir to the benefits of Constantine's immensely significant turn from paganism to Christianity, and there appears to be no factual basis for what the play alleges to have been the emperor's persecution of either Silvester himself or his fellow Christ-

ians at any time, much less during Silvester's tenure as pope, which did not commence until after Constantine's conversion (312) and the issuance of the Edict of Milan (313) confirming the official toleration of Christianity throughout the empire.

37. A conspicuous because isolated ridge rising 2267 feet above sea level at its highest point. It lies a little over 20 miles north of Rome and is visible from it. The fact that Mt. Soracte is celebrated in the poetry of both Vergil and Horace allows the possibility that the author of *Meriasek* was acquainted with classical Latin literature. The greater probability is, however, that he learned of the mountain in *Legenda Aurea,* where it is called Seraptim. The MS reads *seraptyn.*

38. According to later legend, Constantine was stricken with leprosy as a heaven-sent retribution for his doing away with Crispus, his son by his first wife, and subsequently with Fausta, his second wife. Thereupon, the spiritual corruption of the inner man, together with the physical corruption of the outer man, was cleansed by Pope Silvester, who administered absolution and baptism to a repentant Constantine. The play, it should be noted, proceeds under a different set of assumptions as to the root of Constantine's guilt (see n. 36) although the outward manifestation of that guilt, his leprosy, remains the same. History records that Constantine was not baptized until just before his death at Nicomedia in 337, two years after the death of St. Silvester (335).

39. The MS has *Secundus Nuncius* 'Second Messenger,' but since there is no *Primus Nuncius* 'First Messenger,' I have dropped the designation 'Second' as redundant.

40. The MS reads simply *Episcopus* 'Bishop,' to which a second hand has added *poly*. There are several more or less persuasive interpretations of this addition. Stokes ultimately construes Episcopus Poly to mean Bishop of the Province. Nance remarks that the province could be Apulia, nevertheless labeling the character Bishop of Poly. The Cornish scholar, Henry Jenner, is of the opinion that the author or transcriber of *Meriasek* wished to make it plain that this so-called bishop is a pagan, a pagan physician-priest, *i.e.,* a priest of Apollo, construing Cor. *poly* as equivalent to *apol* (see n. 33). In my own view, the substitution of Sol or Soly for Apollo would be least unsatisfactory because that Romanized Mithraic sun-deity is invoked some half-dozen times within the first 1500 lines of the play. The form of the name employed in the present version represents a compromise among the variants considered in this note.

41. The physician's first remarks in this speech are evidently meant to be heard by the audience but not by the other characters on stage. This dramatic device, the aside, was to become a familiar convention of Elizabethan drama and that of later eras, where it was customarily indicated by a stage-direction. Although such directions are not characteristic of medieval Cornish drama, see Harris, *op. cit.,* p. 259, n. 9, for another even earlier (late 14th c. ?) instance of what is patently an aside.

42. Stokes reads this MS stage-direction, which is in Middle English, as follows: *erthyn pott. ye bovke aredy And the urnell enspektad,* which he translates, 'An earthen pot: the book ready; and the urinal (to be) inspected.' For his MS reading, Nance has *erthyn pott, ye bovke aredy, And the urnell and spectac-*

131

lys, which he translates, 'an earthen pot, the book ready, and the urinal and spectacles.' The scribbled notation is difficult to decipher; but Nance's reading, despite its apparent cogency, seems unlikely.

43. See n. 24.

44. The MS again reads *soly* 'Sol' and despite the medical context of the passage, both Stokes and Nance translate the word as naming Sol, not Apollo (see n. 26). I have followed suit although aware that the connotation here clearly points to a major attribute of the sun-god under his earlier name, Apollo, the healer; healer, incidentally, of both body and mind.

45. Because rendered superfluous by First Executioner's opening words, "Hail, my lord Constantine!" the added stage-direction *ad constantinum* 'To Constantine' has been omitted.

46. Present-day Lombardy is a region of N. Italy bordered on the north by Switzerland, on the south by the Po, and lying between the Mincio river to the east, the Ticino to the west. Its regional capital is Milan. At the time *Meriasek* is thought to have been written (second half of the 15th c.?), Lombardy was represented by the Duchy of Milan. Eleven centuries earlier, Constantine the Great divided his empire into dioceses, of which Italy was one. Among the provinces (sub-divisions) of the Diocese of Italy and situated north of the separate Diocese of Rome was that of 4th c. Liguria, then embracing Milan from which Constantine issued his empire-wide edict of religious toleration (see n. 36).

47. The first five lines (1627-31) of this speech are a quite literal rendering of a passage in the Life of St. Silvester as found in *Legenda Aurea* (The Golden Legend) compiled by Jacobus de Voragine. The pertinent passage in the Latin original reads as follows: *Dignitas romani imperii de fonte nascitur pietatis, quae hanc etiam legem dedit, ut capitali sententiae subderetur quiemque in bello aliquem accedisset infantem.*

48. The MS fails to supply a stage-direction to mark the change of scene from earth to heaven. But the celestial location of Jesus has already been established by a suitable rubric between ll. 1287 and 1288, and Heaven is included among the fixed stations on the staging diagram for the first day's play (see Introduction, Staging).

49. Following the removal of the emperor's mask, the MS inserts a non-dramatic passage again quoted from the Life of St. Silvester in *Legenda Aurea,* as follows: *Cum in aquam descendisset baptismatis mirabilis enituit splendor lucis. Sic inde mundus exiuit et christum se vidisse asseruit.* 'When he had gone down into the water of baptism, there shone forth a marvelous splendor of light. So thence he came forth clean and declared that he had seen Christ.' (*Cf.* n. 47).

I have relegated this material to a note because the subsequent speeches of Jesus and Constantine adequately provide its substance.

50. Designation of Part II supplied.

51. The balance of the stage-direction in the MS reads: *And John ergudyn aredy a horse bakke yt was ye Justis wt Constantyn ffor to play ye marchant.* 'And

John Ergudyn, who was the Justice with Constantine, on horseback ready to play the merchant.'

52. See nn. 8 and 28.

53. See n. 28.

54. In naming 8 August as the date of the second annual fair, the play departs from Lectio 5a of the Latin Life of Meriasek (G. H. Doble, "Saint Meriadoc," App. I, in *The Saints of Cornwall,* Part One), which specifies 8 September, *sexto idus Septembris.* Perhaps it was thought better to avoid two fairs in September.

55. The community of Noyal-Pontivy lies a little over 4 miles east of Pontivy. According to Canon Doble (*op. cit.,* p. 129), "a mutilated statue of the saint, dating from the 15th century" is preserved in the sacristy of the parish church, which is likewise held to date from the 15th c. Canon Doble also mentions the presence in the churchyard of "a granite sarcophagus (scheduled as a 'monument historique')...popularly known as the 'Tomb of S. Meriadec.'"

56. Since early in the 14th c., if not before, coastal inhabitants of Cornwall had become known for their sometimes ruthless exercise of what was termed "the right to wreckage" (see F. E. Halliday, *A History of Cornwall,* pp. 131-32). In practice this right was hardly to be distinguished from plunder, made the more tempting by the relatively high incidence of shipwreck on the peninsula's extensive coastline, and in the vicinity of Land's End, for example, its highly treacherous inshore waters before the days of the lighthouse and fog signal. First Outlaw's rough irony seems well calculated to have touched a sympathetic nerve in a Cornish audience of the era.

57. The phrase "from Tamar to Land's End" designates the entire length of Cornwall. For most of its course, the river Tamar forms the eastern boundary of the county, while its westernmost boundary is the Atlantic Ocean at Land's End (see n. 14). The straight-line distance between the two points measures approximately 75 miles.

58. Castle an Dynas, known simply as Dynas (Cor. *dynas* 'castle') until well into the 15th c., is now an historic site located on the downs a short distance east and slightly south of St. Columb Major, Pydar Hundred (East), north central Cornwall. For comment on "hundred," see n. 23. If this stanza is (or reflects) the original, we have another indication of the drama's *terminus a quo.*

59. Far better known for their literary associations than their factual history, the ruins at Tintagel occupy a site of great natural strength and scenic grandeur on the north coast of Cornwall. The earliest remains, estimated by archeologists to date from the 6th c., are those of a Celtic monastery. About 1145 Reginald, Earl of Cornwall, built a Norman castle so situated on a high, thin-waisted promontory as to make the sea a moat. Alternately added to, chiefly on the landward side, and neglected by succeeding earls, the castle came into the possession of Edward the Black Prince when his father, King Edward III, made him Duke of Cornwall in 1337. After Duke Edward's death (1376), Tintagel once more began to deteriorate but before the year 1400 was sufficiently repaired to

serve as a place of detention for political prisoners. Within little more than another two centuries, however, the erosive action of the sea had so encroached upon the isthmus between headland and mainland as to render the castle unusable. It was abandoned in the 16th c., not far from the time that the surviving MS of *Meriasek* came into being. Tintagel had been, as the play maintains, a stronghold of the dukes of Cornwall from before the middle of the 14th c., and its celebrated vestiges are still the property of the duchy at the present time.

It was Geoffrey of Monmouth's *History of the Kings of Britain* (see n. 7) which initiated the traditional association of Tintagel with King Arthur, a tradition carried forward by Malory (*Le Morte Darthur,* 1485), for example, and in the Victorian Age by Tennyson's *Idylls of the King,* first published complete in 1899. From other strains of medieval romance came the tradition that Tintagel once belonged to King Mark of Cornwall and was thereby linked through him with Tristan and Iseult. There is no historical basis for the tie between Arthur and Tintagel, while what evidence there is for King Mark's place of residence in Cornwall points to Castle Dore in the milder southern region of the county rather than a remote, gale-swept headland in the north.

60. See n. 23.

61. In the Latin Lives of such Celtic holy men as St. Petroc, St. Gwinear, and St. Kea, Teudar figures as a pagan tyrant native to Cornwall (see n. 21). But the play departs from this identification when the Duke of Cornwall's chamberlain describes the tyrant as a foreign interloper who "has recently landed on our shores," a description several times confirmed in the course of the ensuing battle of words between the pagan upstart and the Christian duke regnant, including from Teudar's own lips: "However modest my property may have been at home, I have certainly added to it here."

Since, according to the chamberlain, Teudar arrived in Cornwall by sea, one obvious inference would be that he came from Wales, a possibility supported by the matching of his name with that of Rhys ap Teudar (Rhys, son of Teudar), an 11th c. Welshman. For the Welshman's connection with the family line of Conan and/or Conan Meriadoc, see n. 21.

62. The MS reads *lesteudar* 'Teudar's place' (modern spelling, Lestowder), which the Duke's steward locates in Meneage — an old name for the northern part of the Lizard peninsula. Lestowder is in St. Keverne, a parish in the southeast section of the Lizard.

63. MS reads *goddren*. Shown on 20th c. maps as Goodern, it lies less than 3 miles southwest of Truro in the western half of the county, Powder Hundred.

64. An ironic invocation of the Devil, referred to as if he were a pope. To the medieval mind, the points of the compass had spiritual significance, the north being looked upon as Satan's domain. A reflection of this belief may be seen in Cornish churchyards, where the greater part of all burials lie to the south of the church, whose long axis regularly runs from east to west. The like spiritual orientation is preserved in the schematic drawings that accompany the MS text of both the *Ordinalia* and *Beunans Meriasek* (see Introduction, Staging). In this

general context it may be observed that for a person facing east, *i.e.,* toward the altar in a traditional Christian church, north is on his left-hand (*sinister*) side.

65. The name of this supernatural being, for whom no satisfactory identification has yet come to light, appears twice in the play. In this, the first instance (l. 2338), Monfras is called upon as a god (Cor. *du monfras*) by Teudar; in the second instance (l. 3370), cast as a demon, he announces his own name in English: *y say monfras ys my name.* The dramatic context is broadly and mockingly Satanic in each case, reinforcing by implication a medieval view elsewhere stated directly on several occasions in the course of the play: all pagan gods are devils by definition, whatever their adherents may hold them to be.

Without independent evidence one cannot be sure that the name is Monfras rather than Moufras. Monfras, though, has the advantage of offering a Cornish audience a snicker at the demon's name — a possible translation being 'great dung.'

66. The recognition-value of King Mark's name is, of course, as great as that of the other royal supporters claimed by Teudar is small. Mark has been immortalized in medieval romance, his dark history carried down the centuries as the bane of his nephew, Tristan, and his wife, Iseult. But what makes him peculiarly apt as an ally of Teudar, for a perhaps knowledgeable turn-of-the-century author and a possibly knowledgeable audience, is Malory's contemporary representation of him as the most perfidious and treacherous of knights. A decade ago the archeologist Ralegh Radford presided, with Ashley Rowe, at the unveiling of a plaque commemorating his excavation of Castle Dore near Fowey, Cornwall, the traditional headquarters of King Mark. Since then he seems to have somewhat hedged his bets, but Castle Dore is still widely accepted as Mark's base; and nearby is a commemorative stone to Drustan, the son of Cunomorus, the Breton name of Mark.

Christopher Bice in his booklet, *Names for the Cornish* (1970), cites the name Alwar as not actually Cornish but rather a form of the Old English name Aelfwaru, which the *Oxford Dictionary of English Place-Names* finds in the Madron (Cornwall) place-name Alverton, 'Alwar's homestead.' Earlier spelling (1229), Alwarton. The name does appear in the Domesday Book but without useful identification.

King Pygys, according to Henry Jenner, may be an equivalent of Rygys or Ricatus, whose name is incised on an ancient standing cross preserved at Penzance, west Cornwall. Otherwise we cannot even guess at his identity.

If Casvelyn, probably a genuine Cornish name, can be equated with that of Catwallaun, Teudar is looking to aid from Wales, whence King Catwallaun emerged during the 7th c. as a fighter against the English. For a brief time he won his way to the place of "high king from the Thames to the Forth, supreme over British and English underkings" (John Morris, *The Age of Anthur,* p. 240). He was, says Morris (*ibid.,* p. 391), "a barbarian crueller than a pagan."

67. In the original, this stage-direction reads: *gonnys Hic praeliabunt* 'Guns Here they shall fight.' For typographical convenience, I have brought up the additional rubric, *Horse aredy,* from opposite the immediately succeeding line of

the dialogue (2487). It is generally agreed that the word *gonnys* and the phrase, *horse aredy,* are later additions in a different scribal hand, which suggests that the basic text without those embellishments may reflect a time of composition antedating not so much the existence of small cannon or portable firearms in Britain as their availability for use on the stage in as remote an area as Cornwall then was. History records that small cannon were employed on the Continent as early as 1346 during the battle of Crécy, but the first use of small arms, *e.g.,* the shoulder gun, in Britain is assigned to the second battle of St. Albans, 1461.

68. Heading supplied.

69. Constantine's role in delivering a brief prologue to Day II of *Meriasek* may be compared with that of the earlier Roman emperor, Tiberius, who pronounces the epilogue to *Resurrexio Domini,* the final play of the *Ordinalia* trilogy.

70. Nance suggests that the count's name could be emblematic, signifying Count Worldly, from Lat. *globus.* He appears to have arrived at this view through concentration on the burden of the early speeches exchanged between Meriasek and the blind count (blind to spiritual values?), wherein the count emphasizes the great importance of material wealth, which the unworldly saint repudiates.

Put to the test, however, neither the meaning of *globus* in classical or medieval Latin nor the history of the idea of the earth as a globe or sphere gives Nance much, if any, support. Modern English "globe" derives, through Middle English and Old French, from Latin *globus,* but Cassell's *Latin Dictionary* (classical Latin) fails to equate *globus* with 'the world,' the 15th c. English-Latin dictionary *Promptorium Parvulorum* does not list *globus* at all, and neither the Baxter-Johnson *Medieval Latin Word-List* nor du Cange's *Glossarium* supports this connection. Without reference to the earth, all these works (except *Promptorium Parvulorum*) define *globus* to mean 'a round ball, globe, sphere, circle.' To achieve the Nance equivalence, the blind count would have had to be burdened with some such patronymic as Orbis Terrae 'Circle of the World,' yet even this extravagance would not necessarily get us to the heart of the concept of the world as a globe rather than, for example, a shallow disc. True, it was entertained among Greek natural philosophers as early as Aristotle and even earlier, but anything like a popularly held notion of the shape of the earth during the Middle Ages was derived far more from *Genesis* than from, for instance, Ptolemy. Copernicus, Galileo, and Kepler are too late for our purposes.

As for the local, practical circumstances of *Beunans Meriasek* as living theatre, the playwright would, of course, have been aware of the count's name, and Globus is accorded a station on the production diagram for Day II (see Introduction, Staging). Unlike a number of other characters, however, Count Globus does not announce his name to the audience, with the obvious result that the most alert and lettered auditor, receptive to the word, globe, in Latin, English, and Cornish (*pel*), would have had no opportunity to make a connection like that of Nance. Cor. *pel* is here irrelevant, while English "globe" as designating 'the world' does not acquire its earliest entries in the *O.E.D.* until half a century after 1504.

71. Estimated to equal one-half of a knight's annual rent during the reign of Edward I.

72. Only the initial word of this stage-direction, the whole of which appears to be a later addition, can be clearly deciphered in the MS: *ululat* 'he howls.' Stokes construes the remainder to read *en(er)goumenus* 'demoniac.' Nance interprets the MS to have *ululatur et gon & gon,* which he renders 'He howls and a gun is discharged.' The verb *ululare* is not deponent, however, and nance fails to carry over the repetition of *gon* into his translation (typescript, Cornwall County Museum). As a rationale for Nance's working in of an allusion to guns here, see n. 67. His reading seems hardly possible, while Stokes' is a good guess at what the unusually contracted stage-direction intends. The present translation omits all but *ululat,* so that it is the demon, not the demoniac, who howls.

73. Vannes, which takes its name from that of the Veneti, a Gaulish tribe of whose military prowess Julius Caesar writes with respect in his *Commentaries,* is situated at the head of the Gulf of Morbihan on Brittany's south coast. Neither the play nor what was evidently one of its principal sources (a 15th c. *Vita,* see Introduction) mentions the name of the lately deceased bishop of Vannes whom Meriasek is destined to succeed. It remained for the Breton Dominican, Albert Le Grand, in his Life of St. Meriasek (*Vies des saints de la Bretagne armorique,* 1636) to supply the name, which he gives as Saint Hincwteen. Two centuries later, Dom Lobineau, author of *Les Saints de Bretagne* (1836) confirms Hincwteen as the predecessor of Meriasek. Nothing seems to be known of such a saint in other sources.

74. Since in the MS this stage direction calls for the Count's exit several speeches before his share in the scene has been completed, I have moved the rubric forward to a position after l. 2734 instead of l. 2715.

75. MS reads First Messenger. Designation "First" has been dropped because no Second Messenger is involved in this Breton scene nor in the following one at Rome.

76. It may never be known beyond a reasonable doubt precisely what Second Crozier-Bearer is saying in this pair of apparently serio-comic lines (2881-82). But since the major thrust of the present work is literary rather than linguistic, attention will be focused on the crozier-bearer's entire speech as an instance of dramatic characterization and on the presence in l. 2881 of the words *rose noblennou* with their potential contribution to the date-of-composition problem.

Despite the crux, there can be little doubt that Second Crozier-Bearer is struck by what he regards as Meriasek's unaccountable reluctance to accept the prestigious and, in the crozier-bearer's tutored estimation, lucrative office of bishop. His whole-souled acquisitiveness is offended by the saint's other-worldliness, his half-serious, half-comic exasperation seeming to fuse in a pun on the word *noblennou* 'nobles,' simultaneously alluding to high social status and monetary wealth. His apparent venality has, moreover, an analogue in the

Ordinalia where the crozier-bearer to Bishop (*sic*) Caiaphas (Play II, Christ's Passion) lets it be known at an opportune moment that he chances to own a piece of open land suitable for use as a Christian cemetery, which he's quite prepared to sell for the thirty pieces of silver that Judas Iscariot has so lately flung down at the feet of the high priest (Caiaphas).

As an English gold coin formerly valued at 8s.6d., the noble was first minted during the reign of Edward III, *c.* 1345. If, on the other hand, *rose* is to be rendered as 'rose' rather than as a Cornish verb-form meaning 'put' (the latter reading adopted by Stokes from the outset and ultimately by Nance as well), we have rose nobles, an English gold coin of varying value stamped with the image of a rose and first minted by Edward IV, *c.* 1465. Although there are too many variables to permit the establishing of anything like a firm *terminus a quo* based on the time at which these coins were first issued, it seems reasonable to hold that the original composition of ll. 2881-82—and with them, in all probability, a significant portion of the drama as we now have it — could not have taken place before the middle years of the 14th c. at the earliest.

77. To execute this stage-direction in a purely theatrical sense involves no more than a remove of the bishop and his companions from one location on the *platea* to another (see Introduction, Staging). In terms of geographical actuality, the journey is from Vannes (n. 73) to Meriasek's hermitage in the neighborhood of Pontivy (n. 28), about 28 miles to the northwest, rather more than an afternoon stroll whether on foot or horseback. To infer from this circumstance, however, that the playwright is unfamiliar with Breton topography would be ill-advised since in the *Ordinalia,* where very much greater distances are spanned (Jerusalem to Rome, Jerusalem to the Sinai Peninsula), the pertinent rubrics are no less casual in their regard of distance and time requirements. Hence, while the insouciance of this and certain other stage-directions in Peniarth 105 can be taken as symptomatic of unfamiliarity with Breton distances and place-names (the MS fumbles over attempts to settle upon a Cornish equivalent of Vannes, for example), we must await his attempt to specify the site of Meriasek's consecration as bishop in order to expose an outright confusion of one ecclesiastical jurisdiction with another (see following note).

78. Some thirty speeches earlier, the Count of Vannes' messenger to Rome has petitioned Pope Silvester in the name of the Breton lords for authority to consecrate Meriasek as Bishop of Vannes in the cathedral church of that same "fair city." But now the playwright, in following the *Vita* presumably before him, falls into an anachorism causing the Count of Vannes to name St. Samson's church as the site of Meriasek's consecration. In the Middle Ages, the major Breton church dedicated to St. Samson was at Dol. As the *Vita Mercadoci,* Lection 9, attests:...*in urbe Dolensi in Basilica sancti Samsonis Episcopus consecratur* 'He is consecrated bishop in the church of St. Samson in the city of Dol.' In accordance with Breton geography, concerning which the play is inclined to be somewhat vague, Dol lies near the north coast of Brittany, separated from Vannes near the south coast by nearly the full north-south axis of the one-time duchy, yielding a straight-line distance between the two towns of approximately 95 miles.

Conceivably the dramatist would have been less interested in the ecclesiasti-

138

cal and geographical facts, even had he been well aware of them, than in his audience's ability to identify with St. Samson's church near Fowey, Cornwall; or he could have been at least subconsciously aware that long before his day and nearer to what he conceived of as Meriasek's day, Dol enjoyed the status of an archiepiscopal see, that status not reverting to Tours, which is outside Brittany, until 1199.

79. Heading supplied.

80. See Introduction, *Beunans Meriasek* as Drama.

81. A standard source for the outline of the story of Mary and the Woman's Son would have been Jacobus de Voragine's 13th c. *Legenda Aurea*. But an important motive for introducing the legend among the episodes of Day II of the play was undoubtedly of local origin. A contemporary notice of publication of the Stokes edition of *Beunans Meriasek,* appearing in *Revue Celtique* for Dec. 1871-Aug. 1872, observes that the story is included in the play because of the Chapel of Mary of Camborne, the traditionally accepted precursor of Camborne parish church (see nn. 15, 16). The blessing of Mary of Camborne (*banneth maria cambron*) as well as of Meriasek is pronounced on those who have stayed to the close of each Day's performance. The review also remarks that the legend itself has been localized with much invented detail (see Introduction, Sources).

82. I have not followed the distribution of speeches called for by ll. 3232-41 of the MS, which seems to me wrong. My rearrangement parallels that of Nance (typescript, Cornwall County Museum).

83. The only instance in which the play assigns a proper name to the speaking part regularly labeled Drudge or Menial (MS *Calo*). As an anonymous character, *Calo* first enters the action as early as Teudar's futile search for Meriasek in hiding (l. 1023). *Cf.* n. 35.

84. A silver coin formerly worth 4d., first minted 1351-52. *Cf.* n. 76.

85. The equivalent of 3 pounds in late medieval times, perhaps representing for Third Executioner an annual wage in addition to his keep.

86. Compare the status of Monfras here (l. 3370) to that of his earlier invocation by Teudar in l. 2338 (see n. 65).

87. MS reads *voruelys,* which Stokes translates 'Morville' (l. 3415). Nance conjectures that this place-name is a coinage made to rhyme with *elys* 'anointed' in the following line as in "Linkinhorne where the Devil was born / North Hill where he lives still"; although in the Cornish we have an end rhyme, in the English, internal rhyme. I have retained a spelling closer to the Cornish original of this otherwise unidentified name. The east-Cornwall place-name Morval, though spelled Morvelle, Morwelle, etc. in the 15th c., sheds little light.

88. A Satanic blessing (see n. 64).

89. Literally, 'Our holy father from the north part' (see n. 64).

90. In denouncing as a Jew the Tyrant who uniformly swears by Mohammed, King Massen should not be regarded as having made a mistake in the eyes of a medieval Cornish audience. Here, as elsewhere in the play, a Christian recognizes no essential difference between one pagan religion and another since all

are false and their gods — Jove, Apollo, Sol, Mohammed (*sic*) — are therefore devils. The name of Yahweh does not appear in *Beunans Meriasek* (see n. 22).

91. Stokes notes that in the hand which he regards as that of the original scribe, the MS line (3521) begins *Out charlys* 'Out, Charles,' to which another hand adds above the first *Ot ot ot* 'Out, out, out.' I have retained the presumably older wording only. The name Charles aside, Beaumont and Hector were favorite names for hunting dogs, not suitable for Christians in this context.

92. Heading supplied.

93. See n. 17.

94. The original stage-direction reads simply *Descendunt* 'They descend,' to which another hand has added in M.E., *organs or syngyng*. The term *organs* also appears in the King David episode of *Origo Mundi,* where the king is exhorting his numerous musicians to furnish march music. In that instance, it seemed appropriate to interpret *organs* as the equivalent of It. *organetti,* plural of *organetto,* a small, portable organ used in medieval processions (Harris, *op. cit.,* pp. 252-53, n. 14). But in the present context, the meaning 'various instruments of music' as cited from *Cursor Mundi* by *The Oxford Dictionary of English Etymology* seems preferable.

95. More devotional than theatrical in function, these words appear to have been excerpted verbatim from the Latin of the Tréguier Legendary, *Vita Mercadoci Episcopi et Confessoris*, 7 *Junii, Lectio* 6a: "...sumens cibum cum laudibus divinis epulis sentit quotidie se refectum."

96. Heading, including part number, supplied.

97. See nn. 67, 72.

98. It appears that the copyist, in moving from the last line of MS p. 158 to the first on p. 159, has accidentally omitted what Stokes estimates to be "at least three lines" (Stokes, *op. cit.*, p. 234). In his Unified Cornish version of the play (typescript, Cornwall County Museum), Nance undertakes to supply the missing lines as follows: *omma ythof danvenys / gans du ker rag dysky dys / pandra goth dys Sylvester.* ' I am sent hither / By dear God, to inform thee / What behooveth thee, Silvester.' Without prejudice to Nance's contribution, I have elected to conform to the MS as it stands but have inserted an ellipsis as a signal to the reader of a probable omission in Peniarth 105.

99. Though quite possibly inadvertent, this epithet for Mohammed comes nearest to a proper attribution in Islamic terms. See n. 22.

100. See Introduction, *Beunans Meriasek* as Drama.

101. Heading, including part number, supplied.

102. The play itself, not the Breton *Vita*, furnishes this conventional yet dramatically effective setting for Meriasek's dying hours. See Introduction, *Beunans Meriasek* as Drama.

103. A solemn and final confirmation, uttered from his deathbed in Brittany, of Meriasek's principal foundations in Cornwall — a parish church and a Feast Day. Professor Thomas (*op. cit.*, Ch. II) has argued persuasively that an important *raison d'être* for *Beunans Meriasek* may well have been to support "the

sanctity and respectability" of the saint as patron of Camborne church against the claims of his much more widely known rival, St. Martin of Tours (see n. 15). Scattered medieval records between 1329 and 1501 show that the parochial dedication see-sawed between Meriasek and Martin, even producing such a curious anomaly as "The Church of St. Martin or Mereadoc Martin" (1343). Without the reappearance of Peniarth 105 in 1862 and its publication by Stokes in 1872, the eventual rededication of the church to both St. Martin and St. Meriasek, as pronounced by the Bishop of Truro on the 7th Sunday after Easter, 1958, might not have transpired.

104. The balance of this stage-direction, plainly a later addition and out of conformity with the text to follow, has been omitted from the translation but is given here. It reads: *ye holy goste aredy ffro hevyn to fett ye sowle and ye sovle aredy*. A repetition of the same rubric in abbreviated form which follows l. 4342 has likewise been omitted. Redundancies of this kind go to support the opinion that Peniarth 105 was adapted for use as a prompter's or director's copy of the play.

105. The MS reads *descendit* 'he goes down.' But in view of the fact that the Count of Vannes has just called upon his attendant knights to accompany him, I have altered 'he goes' to 'they go.'

106. Because the ostensible setting for this speech is the cathedral at Vannes, I have rendered the manuscript's term, *colgy*, as 'chapter,' *i.e.*, dean and chapter of canons, the traditional governing body of a bishop's church. To a medieval Cornish audience, however, the word *colgy* would have been likely to suggest the most prominent college familiar to them, Glasney Collegiate Church at Penryn. Glasney was a college of secular canons, founded 1265, which endured until the Reformation. Penryn is situated on the south coast of Cornwall near Falmouth. The distance between Penryn and Camborne is about 8 miles. For additional information on Glasney College, see Introduction, Author and Date of Composition; also Thurstan C. Peter, *The History of Glasney Collegiate Church, Cornwall* (Camborne, 1903).

107. The potential significance of this passage does not lodge, to be sure, in the mere fact that Meriasek is reported to have mortified the flesh by wearing a hair shirt next his skin (a fairly common practice among religious ascetics over the centuries) nor the information that his outer garment was "usually of good quality." He was, after all, a bishop, regardless of how reluctantly so at the outset. But when these two more or less contradictory practices are claimed for the same individual, leading us to cast about, under the circumstances of the play, for a conspicuous British rather than continental analogue, the person of Thomas Becket comes to mind. As bishop, martyr, and canonized saint, he was well known for the quiet elegance of his outward apparel, also, like Meriasek, his special sympathy for the poor, and after his murder in the north transept of Canterbury Cathedral (1170), it was reputedly discovered that he wore a hair shirt next his skin. Yet the analogy does not acquire its full persuasivenss in the light of *Beunans Meriasek* until the entire dedication of Glasney College is disclosed: The Collegiate Church of the Blessed Virgin Mary and St. Thomas of Canterbury.

108. Of this dazzling feat of piety, Canon Doble (*op. cit.*, p. 121, n. 24) observes: "This is an attempt to improve on the edifying practice attributed to S. Patrick, who is said to have genuflected 100 times each day and night. The author of the Anglo-Saxon homily on S. Neot appropriates the anecdote for his own hero, and the medieval biographer of S. Meriadec follows his example, increasing the number to 1,000. Dom Lobineau gravely points out that it is a physical impossibility."

109. The literal meaning of the Cor. *boys eleth* is 'angels' food.'

110. Inferring from the context that the singing of a dirge is called for by this stage-direction, Nance suggests as a possible text the opening words of the antiphon in the 1st nocturn at Matins: *Dirige, Domine Deus meus, in conspectu tuo viam meam* 'Direct, O Lord my God, my way in thy sight.' The wording in Latin may be compared with the Vulgate, *Ps.* V, 8. English "dirge" is derived from the imperative of Lat. *dirigere* 'to direct' and from its function in the office.

111. The speech with which the Count of Vannes concludes the play and releases the audience is similar in substance and identical in function to its counterparts at the close of *Origo Mundi* and *Resurrexio Domini*, Days I and III of the *Ordinalia*, as well as *Gwreans an Bys* (Creation of the World), the other Creation drama in the surviving corpus of early Cornish literature. In all four plays, the final speech summarizes the just completed action and bestows blessings upon the spectators. Each calls for music, and three of them — *Resurrexio, Gwreans,* and *Beunans* — invite the audience to dance. Only in the present play, however, are the spectators urged to buy drinks for the financial benefit of the production.

A broadly analogous pronouncement by Nicodemus brings to a close what may one day come to be recognized as Britain's finest medieval Passion Play, *Passio Christi* (Day II of the *Ordinalia*). But here the tone is hushed and high. Nicodemus concludes: "But I ask that you return early tomorrow that you may see how Christ rose, radiant and gentle, from the grave." (Harris, *op. cit.*, p. 175).

Returning to *Meriasek*, it may be noted with what freedom the playwright abandons the dramatic fiction that the saint has been living out his last days in Brittany and allows the Count of Vannes to invoke the blessing of Mary of Camborne, thereby localizing the action-setting for the audience at the imaginative expense of the play. Strictly parochial interests, it would appear, are permitted to dominate at the last.

112. I have left the colophon in the Latin of the original exactly as Stokes transcribed it from the MS. A literal translation, which he omitted, might read: 'Finished by Master Hadton, year of Our Lord 1504.' During the century which has elapsed since Stokes published his edition of the play, a number of versions have been proposed of what he construed to be a single proper name, which he elected to print in all capitals, HADTON. These versions turn on a pair of variables — an initial letter and the option of construing the name as a surname only or as a given name plus a surname. The recorded variants are as follows: Nadton, Radton, Nad Ton, Rad Ton, Rad. (Radolphus) Ton. Since the present work undertakes to be a new translation but not a new edition of Peniarth 105, a discussion of calligraphic niceties would be inappropriate. What can be said is

that a brief inspection of the MS in the National Library of Wales at Aberystwyth and a painstaking examination of a good, positive photostat of it shows that the scribe has written the name (his own?) large, with a distinct separation between two elements, each introduced by a capital letter. The second element, Ton, has never been in question; whether the initial letter of the first element is an "H," an "N," or an "R," like the identity of the person named, may never be definitively resolved. (Also see Introduction, Author and Date of Composition).

SELECTED BIBLIOGRAPHY

Alfoldi, Andrew. *The Conversion of Constantine and Pagan Rome.* Oxford: Clarendon Press, 1948.

Ashe, Geoffrey (ed.) *The Quest for Arthur's Britain.* New York: Praeger, 1968.

Bice, Christopher. *Names for the Cornish.* Padstow: The Lodenek Press, 1970.

Blewett, Richard R. *Celtic Surnames in Cornwall.* 2 vols. MS, Cornwall County Museum.

Borlase, William. *Observations on the Antiquities, Historical and Monumental, of the County of Cornwall.* London: W. Jackson, 1754.

Borlase, William Copeland. *The Age of the Saints.* 2nd ed. Truro: J. Pollard, 1895.

Brengle, Richard L. *Arthur, King of Britain.* New York: Appleton-Century-Crofts, 1964.

Brown, H. Miles. *The Church in Cornwall.* Truro: Oscar Blackford, 1964.

Burch, Vacher. *Myth and Constantine the Great.* London: Oxford, 1927.

Burckhardt, Jacob. *The Age of Constantine the Great.* New York: Pantheon Books, 1949.

Camden, William. *Britannia.* Edited by Edmund Gibson. 2nd ed. London: Awnsham Churchill, 1722.

Chadwick, Nora K. *Early Brittany.* Cardiff: University of Wales, 1969.

Coleman, Christopher Bush. *Constantine the Great and Christianity.* New York: Columbia University, 1914.

Doble, Gilbert H. *Four Saints of the Fal.* "Cornish Saints" Series, No. 20. Exeter: Printed by Sydney Lee, 1929.

_____.*Saint Gwinear, Martyr.* Long Compton: The King's Stone Press, n.d.

_____.*Saint Petrock, Abbot and Confessor.* Long Compton: The King's Stone Press, n.d.

_____.*The Saints of Cornwall, Part I.* Chatham: Printed for the Dean and Chapter of Truro by Parrett & Neves, 1960.

Elliott-Binns, L. E. *Medieval Cornwall.* London: Methuen, 1955.

Fleetwood, Bishop. *Chronicon Preciosus...* Printed for T. Osborne, in Gray's-Inn, 1745.

Geoffrey of Monmouth. *History of the Kings of Britain.* Translated by Sebastian Evans, revised by Charles W. Dunn. New York: E. P. Dutton, 1958.

The Golden Legend of Jacobus de Voragine. Translated by Granger Ryan and Helmut Ripperger. London: Longmans, Green & Co., 1941.

Gontard, Friedrich. *The Popes*. Translated by A. J. and E. F. Pieler. London: Barrie & Rockliff, 1964.

Gover, J. E. B. *The Place-names of Cornwall*. (Typescript). Cornwall County Museum. [1948.]

Halliday, F. E. *A History of Cornwall*. London: Duckworth, 1959.

Harris, Markham. *The Cornish Ordinalia*. Washington, D. C.: The Catholic University of America Press, 1969.

Henderson, Charles. *Cornish Church Guide and Parochial History of Cornwall*. Truro: D. Bradford Barton, 1964.

_____. *A History of the Parish of Constantine in Cornwall*. Edited by G. H. Doble. Printed for the Royal Institution of Cornwall by the King's Stone Press, Long Compton, 1937.

Histoire de la Bretagne. Publiée sous la direction de Jean Delumeau. (Univers de la France). Toulouse: Edouard Privat, 1969.

Jenner, Henry. "Castle-an-Dinas and King Arthur." *88th Report of the Royal Cornwall Polytechnic Society*. (New Series, Vol. 4, Part iv, 1921-22), 83-101.

_____. *The Cornish Drama (IV, Ordinale de Vita Sancti Mereadoci, 127-65)*. MS, Cornwall County Museum.

_____. *The Immigration of the Irish Missionary Saints into Cornwall in the Late 5th and Early 6th Centuries*. MS, Cornwall County Museum.

_____. *King Teudar of Cornwall: A Study in Cornish Hagiology*. MS, Cornwall County Museum.

_____. "Perran Round and the Cornish Drama." *79th Report of the Royal Cornwall Polytechnic Society* (1912), 38-44.

_____. *The Sources of the Cornish Dramas*. MS, Cornwall County Museum.

Leake, Stephen Martin. *An Historical Account of English Money, from the Conquest to the Present Time*. 3d ed. London: Printed for R. Foulder *et al.*, 1793.

Liber Landavensis. Translated by W. J. Rees. Llandovery: Published for the Welsh MSS Society, 1860.

Liverpool, Charles, First Earl of. *A Treatise on the Coins of the Realm*. London: Effingham Wilson, 1880.

Memento des sources hagiographiques de l'histoire de Bretagne. Rennes: L. Buhon-Roult, éditeur, 1918.

Morris, John. *The Age of Arthur*. New York: Charles Scribner's Sons, 1973.

Nance, R. Morton. "The Criss-Cross Row." *Old Cornwall*. Vol. 1, No. 5 (1927), 9-13.

_____. Bewnans Meriasek in Unified Spelling. (Typescript). Cornwall County Museum.

Ordinale de Vita Sancti Mereadoci, Episcopi et Confessoris. MS. Peniarth 105, National Library of Wales.

Norden, John. *Speculi Britannie Pars: A Topographical and Historical Description of Cornwall*. London: William Pearson, 1728.

Peter, Thurstan C. *The History of Glasney Collegiate Church*. Camborne: Camborne Printing & Stationery Co., 1903.

Petrie, W. M. Flinders. "Neglected British History." *Proceedings of the British*

Academy, VIII. Published for the British Academy by Humphrey Milford, Oxford University Press, n.d.

Pitre-Chevalier. *La Bretagne ancienne et moderne.* Paris: W. Coquebert, [1844].

Radford, C. A. Ralegh. "Report on the Excavations at Castle Dore." *Journal of the Royal Institution of Cornwall* (New Series, Vol. I, Appendix, 1951), 1-119.

Raison du Cleuzion, Alain. *La Bretagne de l'Origne à la Réunion.* 2nd ed. Saint-Brieuc: Imprimerie-Librairie de René Prud'Homme, 1914.

Schoff, Philip and Wace, Henry (eds.) *A Select Library of Nicene and Post-Nicene Fathers of the Christian Church.* Second Series, Vol. I. New York: The Christian Literature Company, 1890.

Southern, Richard. *The Medieval Theatre in the Round.* London: Faber and Faber, 1957.

Stokes, Whitley (ed.) *The Life of Saint Meriasek, Bishop and Confessor.* London: Trübner, 1872.

_____. Henry Jenner annotated copy, Cornwall County Museum.

_____. R. Morton Nance annotated copy, Cornwall County Museum.

_____. Whitley Stokes annotated copy, University College, London.

Thomas, A. C. "The Folk-Lore of the Camborne District." *117th Report of the Royal Cornwall Polytechnic Society* (1950), 26-37.

Thomas, Charles. *Christian Antiquities of Camborne.* St. Austell: H. E. Warne, 1967.

Vallaux, C., Waquet, H., Dupouy, A., and Chasse, C. *Visages de la Bretagne.* Collection 'Provinciales,' Éditions des Horizons de France. Paris, 1940.